中华敬老故事精选

Selected China Stories of Elder-Respecting

主编 李宝库

副主编 陆颖

中华茶养生事精粹

主编　李宝庆
副主编　胡兰

谨以此书献给收养中国弃孤儿童的父母们

Sincerely present this book to the parents
who adopt abandoned children
and orphans in China

弘扬中华民族美德，
扶助孤儿健康成长，
开展涉外收养工作，
增进各国人民感情。

李立国
2004年8月18日

李立国：民政部副部长

To carry forward national virtues,
To help orphans thrive,
To develop intercountry adoption program,
And to promote friendship between the peoples
of all countries.

Li Liguo
August 18, 2004

Li Liguo: vice-minister of the Ministry of Civil Affairs

敬老心语

李宝库

孝亲敬老是人的高尚品德的一面镜子。

关爱今天的老年人，就是关爱明天的自己。

只有孝敬自己的父母，才能得到子女的孝敬。

怎样关爱自己的儿女，就应该怎样关爱自己的父母。

只有像关爱自己的父母一样关爱公婆，才可能使自己的父母得到同样的关爱。

大象无形，大音稀声，大爱无言。父母的大爱，常在不言之中。中华传统，尊师如父，成功者，永远不要忘记传道授业解惑之人。忠和孝都是人的爱心的表现。孝是小家之爱，忠是大"家"之爱；孝是忠的基础，忠是孝的升华。当忠孝不能两全时，为国尽忠，也就内含了为父母尽孝之德。

孝亲敬老，是中华民族的传统美德，是人伦道德的基石，是中华文化的瑰宝。她历经几千年历史大潮的洗礼，愈发显得光彩夺目。在我国新的历史时期，弘扬我们的传统美德，对于和谐家庭、稳定社会、富强国家，实现中华民族的伟大复兴，有着十分重要的意义。根据古代敬老文献、当代民间习俗和几年来的工作实践，我收集整理了这份"敬老心语"。适逢中英文版的《中华敬老故事》出版，就以此作为本书的序言，献给海外一切热心中华孝道的朋友们，献给一切黄皮肤、黑头发的可爱的孩子们。

二〇〇四年五月二十五日
于中国北京

Heartfelt Words on Respecting Elders

By Li Baoku

Esteeming relatives and respecting elders indicate one´s magnificent morality like a mirror.

To care for elders of today is to care for ourselves of tomorrow.Only if you respect your parents will your children respect you.You should care about your parents as how you care about your children.

Only if you treat your parents−in−law as your own parents can your own parents be treated in the same way.

Huge scene may not have a shape; big sound may not be loud and great love may not be spoken out. The great love of parents is usually expressed wordlessly.

It is the Chinese tradition to respect your teacher as your father. Successful people should never forget their teachers who transmit wisdom, impart knowledge, and resolve doubts for them.

Both loyalty and filial piety are reflections of love. Filial piety is the love for your own small family, while loyalty is the love for the big family of your country. Filial piety is the basis of loyalty, while loyalty is the sublimation of filial piety. When contradictions emerge between them, keep an utter loyalty to your country. The loyalty contains your very filial piety to your family.

Esteeming relatives and respecting elders is a traditional virtue of the Chinese nation, the cornerstone of the human morality and a treasure of the Chinese culture. Baptized with the tide of the history of thousands of years, it becomes even more brilliant. In a new stage of Chinese history, to carry forward our traditional virtues is of big significance with the family harmonization, social stability, national prosperity and a great rejuvenation of the Chinese nation. According to some documents on elder—respecting in ancient times, folk customs of the present days and by my own work experiences of these years, I collected and organized the "Heartfelt Words on Respecting Elders". It happens to be on the occasion of the publication of the book Chinese Stories of Elders—Respecting of Chinese and English editions, so I would like to use this essay as the prologue of the book and devote it to all the friends abroad who are enthusiastic in Chinese filial piety and to all the lovely children with yellow skin and black hair.

May 25th, 2004
Beijing, China

前　言

　　中国政府高度重视孤残儿童的权益保护，采取兴办社会福利机构集中抚育、开展家庭寄养、积极推动国内收养和涉外收养等多种安置方式，为孤残儿童提供尽可能好的生活环境。正是在这样的背景下，中国的涉外收养工作逐步开展起来，并随着改革开放政策的逐步推广和国际交往的日益扩大，得到进一步发展。《中华人民共和国收养法》和《外国人在中华人民共和国收养子女登记办法》的相继颁布，为中国涉外收养工作的开展提供了法律依据，保障了这项工作的正常进行。目前，中国已与澳大利亚、比利时、冰岛、加拿大、丹麦、芬兰、法国、爱尔兰、荷兰、新西兰、挪威、西班牙、瑞典、英国、美国、新加坡等16个国家建立了收养合作关系，保持收养事务往来的收养机构有170多个。来自这些国家的众多收养家庭从中国收养了孩子，也由此与中国结下了割不断的情缘。

　　这些收养家庭真心地爱着与自己没有血缘关系的中国孩子，为他们提供无微不至的照顾，病残儿童还得到及时治疗和康复。"儿童应生长在一个充满幸福、亲爱和理解的家庭环境中"，这是海牙公约的宗旨，也是所有帮助中国孤残儿童的人们的共同心愿。在此，我们要感谢不远万里，不辞辛苦，到中国收养孩子的父母们。正是他们无私的爱，使这些原本不幸的孩子变得幸福，原本孤独的孩子重获家庭温暖。

　　本书搜集了41个感人至深、催人泪下、富于哲理的中华敬老故事，蕴涵了父母关爱子女、子女孝敬父母的至情至爱。"夫孝，德之本也。"这些中华古训，历经几千年，依然为中华民族所信仰和尊崇，依然是中国人积极倡导的行为准则，是调节代际关系、促进家庭和睦、推动社会文明进步的民族瑰宝。

　　我们谨以此书献给收养父母和他们收养的中国孩子。希望收养父母能给孩子讲讲书中的故事。我们知道，有许多收养父母都让他们的孩子继续学习中国文化，继续保留中国传统，学中文、过中国节日、穿中国传统服装等等点点滴滴的事情，为孩子系上了中国结，留住了中国根。我们深信，通过书中这些真实、感人的故事，中国被收养的孩子将能了解中华民族孝亲敬老的传统美德，更深地体会收养父母对他们付出的爱，将来也会以同样的爱回报养育他们的父母。情浓于血，爱无国界。只要有亲情，就有家庭的温暖；只要有爱，就有人性的光辉。愿这本书不仅令你了解中华孝道，更让你净化心灵，收获真情与感动，更深刻地体会做人的道理。

　　　　　　　　　　　　　　　　　　　　中国收养中心

　　　　　　　　　　　　　　　　　　　　二○○四年六月十七日

Preface

The Chinese government attaches great attention to the protection of the interests of the orphans and handicapped children. It provides those children with best possible living environment by setting up social welfare institutions, nurturing children in a concentrated manner, developing family foster care system, making active promotion of different types of placement like domestic adoptions and international ones. With such a background, the international adoption program had been developed step by step and made a further progress with the gradual promotion of the opening-up and reforming policy and an increasing expansion of international communication. *The Adoption Law of the People's Republic of China and the Implementation Measures for the Adoption of Children by Foreigners in the People's Republic of China* were promulgated one after another, which equipped China's international adoption program with a legal foundation and secured it with a good prosecution. To date, China has established adoptive cooperation with 16 countries which are Australia, Belgium, Canada, Denmark, Finland, France, Iceland, Ireland, Netherlands, New Zealand, Norway, Singapore, Spain, Sweden, UK, and US, and keeps communications on adoption matters with more than 170 adoption agencies. Numerous adoptive families from these countries adopt children in China; therefore they have made a strong connection with China.

These adoptive families love the Chinese children who indeed have no kin with them with all their hearts. They take the greatest care of the children, among whom the ill and handicapped receive timely medical treatment and rehabilitation. It is the recognition in the Hague Convention that the child "should grow up in a family environment, in an atmosphere of happiness, love and understanding", which is also a common wish of all people who helped and are helping the Chinese orphans and handicapped children. Herein, we would love to give our gratitude to the parents who come all that distance and spare no efforts to travel to China to do their adoptions. Thanks to their selfless care, those children who used to be ill-fated turn to be happy, and those who used to be lonely regain the family warmth.

This book contains true feelings and love of parents caring children and children showing filial respect to parents with 41 Chinese stories of elders–respecting, which are deeply–moving, weepy and richly–philosophical. Chinese old sayings such as "Filial obedience is the source of virtue" have been passed on for thousands of years, and they are still believed, worshiped and regarded as the code of conduct advocated positively by the people of China. They are national treasures that can adjust the relations between different generations, promote a family harmony and accelerate the development of social civilization.

We sincerely present this book to the adoptive parents and

the children they adopted in China, and hope the parents will tell the stories in this book to their children. We know that many parents help their children continue to have Chinese culture and keep the Chinese tradition. They let the children study Chinese, celebrate Chinese festivals, wear Chinese traditional costumes and do many other things, thus to make a Chinese knot on the children and retain their root of China. We firmly believe that, with these real and heart-warming stories, the adopted Chinese children will be able to have some knowledge of the traditional virtue of showing filial respect to parents and the elders and have a deeper taste of the care that the adoptive parents give to them, and repay their parents the same care in times to come.

Love is stronger than blood. Love is without boundaries. So long as one has family feelings, he or she would have warmth. So long as one has love, he or she would have the glory of human nature. Hope this book will not only acquaint you with the filial duty in Chinese culture, but also purify your soul, let you be moved, harvest true feelings, and have a better understanding of the way to be a good person.

China Center of Adoption Affairs
June 17, 2004

目录 Contents

目录 Contents

目录 Contents

目录 Contents

目录 Contents

跪乳图

牛耕马负犬守门
羊羔跪乳知母恩
人若不思养育情
应忆初牛羊心
二〇〇三年春天画羊羔跪乳
邢振龄并诗

母子情

母亲是"钟"

母亲像只散了架的钟，终于停下了脚步。我不禁回想起母亲曾为我当钟的悠悠往事。

读小学时，家里没有钟，为了能按时到校，我每天到近邻王麻子的烟酒店门口，望一眼货架上的旧闹钟。一次，我又去看钟，王麻子没好气地冲我说："想看钟，买个回家好好看！"这句话深深地刺痛了我的心，我噙着眼泪跑回家，放声大哭。母亲边替我擦眼泪边说："孩子，咱人穷志不穷，以后别去他家看钟了，妈给你报时。"

上了中学后，时间就更紧了。我家住在东市区，每天天不亮就要步行到位于中市区的二中上早自习课。为了不让我迟到，母亲这只"钟"更是不知疲倦地工作着。

每当夜幕降临，母亲一面在油灯下做着针线活，挣点钱补贴家用，一面为我守夜计时。夜间，她要不时地跑到屋外，抬头望望启明星移到了什么位置，侧耳听听远处的雄鸡已啼了几遍，再确定是否该喊我起床。每当我起床后看见母亲那充满血丝的双眼，胸中便涌动着阵阵酸楚："母亲呀，您真是一只催人奋进的钟，儿子决不会辜负您的期望。"望星空，听鸡鸣，这是一种原始的计时方法，母亲往往判断得八九不离十，使我从未迟到过。

但是母亲也有失误的时候。一天夜里，天上阴云密布，星星始终未露脸儿，远处雄鸡又死绝了似的未叫一声，母亲沉不住气了，忙催我："天不早了，快起来吧！"我匆匆穿上衣服，洗一把脸，背上书包，一路小跑向学校奔去。到了校门口，只见大门紧闭着，传达室传出了"当、当"两下钟声，原来才凌晨两点。我犹豫了："回家吧，万一睡过点了岂不冤枉？不回吧，还能在校门口站到天亮？"阵阵寒风吹得我直打哆嗦。干脆，跑步吧。我在马路上来回不停地跑，直到天亮学校开门。放学回家后，母亲听完我的叙述，把我紧紧搂在怀里，滚烫的泪珠掉在我的额上。第二天放学回家，我一眼看到桌上摆着一只崭新的小闹钟。我又看看母亲，见她躺在床上，面色苍白。爱说话的小妹道出了实情："妈妈卖了血，买了钟。"我顿时鼻子一酸，泪水夺眶而出。

母亲的一生确实如钟，为了儿女长大成为有用之才，她一刻不停地奔忙着。每每想起这些，我觉得总有一种无形的力量在鞭策着我也要像钟一样，在人生道路上争分夺秒地工作，奋力向前，向前……

（文 林森）

【点评】

母亲为了孩子，可以舍得一切，奉献一切，忍受一切，充当一切，包括为儿子上学做一只报时的"钟"。作为子女应该怎样回报母亲呢？

My Mother, My "Clock"

Mother is like a clock that has been pulled to pieces and stops in the end. I could not but recall the past when my mother served as my clock.

When I was in elementary school, there was no clock in my home. In order to arrive at school on time, I would peep into Wang MaZi's grocery store in my neighborhood every day to have a look at the old alarm clock on the rack. Once when I went to look at the clock, the grocery owner said to me angrily, "Why not buy yourself a clock so that you can look at it at home！" I felt hurt deep in my heart. I ran home with tears in my eyes and burst out crying. Wiping my tears, my mother said, "My boy, though we are poor, we have high moral integrity. Don't go there anymore. I'll tell you the time."

After I entered the middle school, time became even more important to me. I lived in the Dongshi District and I had to get up before sunrise to walk to No. 2 Middle School in the Zhongshi District for morning study. To keep me on time, my mother worked as a clock without stopping.

When night fell, my mother stayed up late at night to keep the time for me while doing her needlework for some extra money. She sometimes went out to see where the morning star moved or tried to hear the cock crow, and then decided when to call me. Every time I got up and saw her red eyes, I felt deeply grateful and said to her, "Mother, you are such an encouraging clock that I won't disappoint you." Though she used the most primitive ways of telling time by looking at the stars and listening to the cock crow, she was quite accurate. I was never late for school.

But sometimes my mother would make mistakes too. One night, dark clouds gathered in the sky and no stars could be seen. The cock also seemed to be dead, making no sound. Losing her patience, my mother said to me, "Come on, it is time to get up." I rushed to put on my clothes, washed my face, grabbed my school bag, and ran to school. When I came to the school gates, they were still shut. Then there came the sound "dang dang" from the clock striking two in the reception room. It turned out to be only two o'clock in the morning. I was in dilemma, if I went home to sleep, I might oversleep. If not, would I just stand here till sunrise? I was shivering in the cold winds. Then I decided to jog along the road back and forth until the school gates opened. When I returned home after school and told my mother about it, she clasped me tightly in her embrace, warm tears rolling off her cheeks to my forehead. When I returned home the following day, I saw a brand new alarm clock on my table. I looked at my mom and she was lying in her bed, looking pale. My little sister told me that she sold her blood and bought the clock. Hearing this, I could not but burst into tears.

The life of my mother is really like a clock. To help her children grow up, she worked without stopping all her life. Every time I think of this, I feel an intangible force encouraging me to go forward in my life, as a clock, forward, forward...

(Lin Sen)

【Comment】

Mother can sacrifice everything, dedicate all her energy, bear everything and act as everything for the sake of her children, including serving as a clock to ensure that her son gets to school on time. What can children give in return?

一袋父母 "心"

豫南劳改农场一个太康犯人，看到别人的家属隔三差五地来看望，非常羡慕。于是一封又一封地向家中写信，每月几块钱的"劳改金"全都用在买信封和邮票上了。可是，半年多过去了，家里也没人来看他。他急了，给家里发了一封"绝交信"。

他的爹娘就他这一个娃儿，其实早就想来看他，只因家中实在太穷，几十元的路费也借不来。老两口接到"绝交信"再也坐不住了，经过一番认真考虑和准备，决定去探望儿子。

他们把自家的板车弄了出来，仔细检查轮胎有没有漏气。感到没啥大问题了，就把家里仅有的一条稍新点的被子铺到车上，然后向劳改农场出发了。

在路上，老两口始终保持着一个拉车、另一个在车上休息，谁累了谁歇，但板车不能停。他爹不忍心让他娘累着，就埋头拉车，被催得急了，才换班歇一歇。因为路远，他爹的鞋子很快磨破了。从清早到晚上，一直走到天黑得看不清东西，才找根木棍把车一支，两人在大野地里睡一会儿。等天刚蒙蒙亮，又开始赶路……就这样，100多里路程，他们走了三天两夜才到达。

　　得知老两口徒步从百里外的家乡来看儿子，农场所有的人都为之震惊了！尤其看到从那双磨破的鞋中探出的黑色脚趾，围观的犯人们都掉泪了。连管教干部也转过头去，用手擦拭着眼睛。这时，只听"扑通"一声，太康犯人重重地在爹娘面前跪了下去！

　　见此情景，人们赶忙上前去拉他，可无论如何，他就是跪地不起。管教干部发话了："谁也别拉他，就让他跪着，他也该跪跪了！"说完，撇下太康犯人，拉着两个老人进了干部食堂，并吩咐做饭的师傅赶快做些汤面。片刻工夫，满满两大碗汤面端上来。看样子老两口真是饿坏了，也没过多推让，也不往椅子上坐，原地一蹲，便大口大口吃起来。三下五除二就把面条吞个精光，连汤都没剩一点，直吃得满头大汗。

　　一般家属来看望只有半个小时，管教干部觉得老两口来一次不易，就尽量放宽时间。两位老人无声地端详了娃儿好久，才依依不舍地上路了。临走前，费力地从板车上拖下一只大麻袋，说是娃儿在这里干活改造，怕他吃不饱，给留点吃的。

　　看着老人一步三回头渐渐远去的背影，太康犯人还在地上跪着，满脸泪痕。大家心里一阵发酸，同时也纳闷，这么一大麻袋都是什么吃的？既然他们带了食物，怎么会饿成那样？两个犯人上前帮忙抬起那麻袋。一不小心麻袋的扎口开了，只见一个个圆圆的东西滚了一地，仔细一瞧，竟都是馒头，足足有几百个！大的、小的、圆的、扁的，没有一个重样的。显然，这是一袋"百家饭"，而且这些馒头都已被晾得半干了。

　　不敢想像，老两口是怎样挨家挨户地讨要了这么多馒头！怕儿子一时吃不完坏了，他们一人拉车，一人在车上晾晒馒头……他们哪里知道，劳改农场的饭菜放量吃，这儿的"杠子馍"，一个就有一斤重。

这麻袋里装的哪里是馒头啊，分明是一袋鲜活的父母心！

只听得太康犯人一声撕心裂肺的哭喊："爹、娘，我改！"

（文　杨小海）

【点评】

儿子寄给父母的是一信袋"怨恨"，父母带给儿子的是一袋"爱心"。浓浓父母情，融化了铁石心肠。

A Bag of Love

A prison inmate from Taikang at Yunan Reform—Through-Labor Farm was full of admiration when he saw that other inmates' families often came to see them. He wrote one letter after another to his parents, spending almost all his monthly allowance on envelopes and stamps. But more than six months passed and no family members came to see him. He was so furious that he wrote another letter to break off relations with his family.

In fact, because he was the only son in his family, his parents had wanted to see him very much. But the family was too poor to afford the travel expense. When the old couple received their son's last letter, they could not wait any longer. After they thought about it carefully and prepared well, they decided to see their son.

They pulled out their flat board cart and checked the tires. Finding no problems with the cart, they put the only fairly new quilt that they could find at home on the cart and set off.

During the way to the farm, the old couple kept going with one pulling the cart and the other resting on the cart. Whoever felt tired could rest, but the cart could never stop. The husband could not bear

房前燕子
飛秋去春
還回
父母憑窗望
我兒何日歸

甲申正三哥

烏思隱念天涯游子的父母之心

to let his wife get tired, so he kept pulling and didn't shift with his wife until he was urged to rest. It was a long way to go and he wore out his shoes very fast. From morning till night, they kept going till it was too dark to see anything ahead. Then they found a stick to support the cart and they slept for a while in the wild field. At sunrise they set off again. It took them three days and two nights to travel more than 50 kilometers to get to the farm.

All the people on the farm were surprised to see the old couple pulling the poor cart to see their son from 50 kilometers away. Some inmates found their eyes wet with tears when seeing the black toes from the worn-out shoes. The prison officials turned their heads and wiped their wet eyes. Then a heavy sound was heard and the son of the old couple knelt down in front of his parents.

Seeing this, some people went to pull him up, but he couldn't be budged. One official said to them, "Do not pull him. Let him kneel there. He needs to do it." Then he helped the old couple into the canteen and ordered some noodles for them. A moment later two big bowls of noodles were ready. The couple must have been very hungry. They squatted down and started to eat in big mouthfuls. In no time, they finished the noodles with no soup left, sweat on their faces.

Usually, a family meeting lasts no more than half an hour. But this time, thinking of the long way the old couple had come, the official permitted them to have a longer meeting. The old couple looked at their son for a long while without saying anything. They were reluctant to leave the farm. Before they left, they pulled off a big bag from the cart, telling their son that they had brought some food for him in case that he didn't have enough to eat after his labor.

Seeing his parents so reluctant to leave, the prison inmate knelt down again, tears rolling down his cheeks. Other people felt sad and also wondered: what had the old couple left with their son? Why had they been hungry, since they had a whole bag of food? Two prison inmates came up to help carry the bag. The bag opened suddenly and out came lots of round things. It turned out that there were several hundred buns, big ones, small ones, round ones, and flat ones. None of them was of the same shape. Obviously this was a bag of food begged from neighbors. Most of the buns were already half dried.

It was hard to imagine how the old couple begged for so many buns from door to door! Afraid the buns might go bad, they dried those buns while pulling the cart... What they didn't know was that the prison inmates on the farm could eat as much as they wanted. The buns they had on the farm could weigh about half a kilogram each.

What were in the bag were not the buns, but love from his parents!

The boy cried his heart out: "I will repent, Father and Mother!"

(Yang Xiaohai)

【Comment】

The son sent to his parents a bag of "complaints," but his parents sent him a bag of love in return. Parental love has melted the son's "heart of stone".

少女捐肾救父

2003年1月24日下午3时30分，在广西桂林解放军181医院接待室里，25岁的韩峰和23岁的弟弟韩磊眼睛发肿，哽咽不止。此时，他们的妹妹——18岁的广西钦州市小学教师韩瑜正在手术室里，再过一会儿，医生将把她的肾摘下移植到父亲的体内。

事情的原委是这样的：

46岁的父亲被医院诊断为慢性肾炎晚期，2000年初，转为尿毒症。

父亲的病情牵动着儿女们的心。一个偶然的机会，韩峰、韩磊和韩瑜三兄妹从报纸上了解到：如果家庭提供肾源，不仅可以节约很多医疗费，而且更容易"种植"。

"我是老大，我有责任捐肾给爸爸。"25岁的韩峰当仁不让，首先提出来为父捐肾。

"不行！我也是儿子，凭什么我就不能捐？"23岁的弟弟韩磊说。

"女儿也是父亲亲生的，要捐就捐我的。"18岁的韩瑜此言一出，立即招致两个哥哥强烈反对，理由是："你年龄小，一个女孩子家，摘掉一个肾将来怎么嫁人？"

韩瑜说："那这样吧，我们三人签订一个君子协定，谁的肾好谁就捐给爸爸。"这个提议得到两个哥哥的积极响应，当即草拟了一份协议，三兄妹在协议书后面郑重签名。协议书签订后，韩峰和韩磊对妹妹耍了一招：他们没有遵守协议中三人同去检查身体的约定，哥俩偷偷提前跑到医院做检查，目的是"先做为快"，以此堵死妹妹的换肾之路。岂料这次检查让哥俩大失所望，韩峰的左肾偏小，韩磊携带有乙肝病毒，他俩的肾都不能移植。

此时，妹妹也悄悄去医院做了检查。结果是：双肾十分健康！

"我赢了！我赢了！"韩瑜兴奋地直奔回家，迫不及待地将诊断报告往哥哥面前一扬，"哈哈！你俩别指望和我争了！"

三兄妹争相为父捐肾的消息，使父亲大为震惊。特别是自己的千金宝贝要求"割肾救父"，让他更没法接受。他坚决拒绝女儿的孝心："阿瑜，你的心意爸爸领了，但说什么我也不会要你的肾。割掉女儿身上的肉，比剐割我的心还难受啊！"

"不！"韩瑜跪在父亲的病床前，眼泪哗哗地直掉，"爸爸，我的生命是你给的，我现在只割舍一个肾算什么呀？如果你不答应女儿的请求，我会一生不安啊！"韩瑜跪在地上"要挟"父亲："若不接受我的肾脏移植，我已写好了辞职书，将日日夜夜陪跪在父亲病床前……"

半个小时过去了，两个小时过去了，母亲、哥哥和亲友们纷纷赶来劝她，但韩瑜仍双膝跪地不起，她的膝盖磨出了血丝，她咬着牙全身开始发抖。父亲再也忍受不住女儿的"跪刑"，放声痛哭："我的乖女儿呀！你快起来吧……"父亲点头默认了女儿"割肾救父"的决定。

院方为全国首例少女"割肾救父"的孝心所感动，特意减免了一些费用。有些药品厂家也愿为韩瑜的父亲免费供药。韩瑜的手术采用的是国内较先进的"腹腔镜",在腹部开一个小口,然后用一种特制的工具将肾取出。

18年前,父亲给了女儿一个自然生命。今天,十几分钟的手术,女儿让父亲"获得新生"。

(文 阿成)

【点评】

三兄妹争相为父捐肾,特别是妹妹跪地求父的真诚孝心,催人泪下,感天动地。

To Save Her Father

At 3:30 pm on January 24, 2003, in the reception room of the Guangxi Guilin No. 181 PLA Hospital, 25-year-old Han Feng and his 23-year-old brother Han Lei were sobbing, eyes swollen. Their younger sister Han Yu, an 18-year-old teacher at Qinzhou City Primary School of Guangxi Province, was in the operation room. In a moment, she would have one of her kidneys removed and transplanted into her father's body.

This is how it started:

Their father, 46, was diagnosed with chronic nephritis of later period and in early 2000, it changed into uremia.

His illness made his three children very uneasy. By chance the children learned from a newspaper that if family members could donate a kidney, it would not only save a great deal of the operation fees, but the transplant could also be more successful.

"I'm the eldest. It is my duty to donate my kidney to Father." 25-year-old Han Feng was the first to stand out.

"No. I am his son too. Why can't I donate? " 23-year-old Han Lei followed.

"I'm a girl, but I am also a child of our father. It would be better for me to donate my kidney," said 18-year-old Han Yu. Hearing that, her two brothers objected right away. "You're too young to donate a kidney. Furthermore, you are a girl. How could you get married with only one kidney?"

Han Yu said, "there is a way to solve this problem. We three children will sign a gentleman's agreement. Whoever has the best kidney donates." The suggestion was supported right away by the two brothers, so they drafted an agreement and signed their names. After signing, Han Feng and Han Lei broke the stipulation that the three children would go together to have their kidneys checked. Instead, they went to the hospital without their sister in order to increase their chances over her. To their disappointment, the examination showed that neither of them could donate a kidney, as Han Feng's left kidney was too small and Han Lei was a hepatitis B virus carrier.

Then Han Yu went to have her kidneys checked. She had two healthy kidneys!

"I won! I won!" Han Yu ran home with excitement, showing the examination report to her brothers right away. "Ha! You two don't have any chance against me now!"

Their father was very surprised when he heard this. He couldn't bear to have his children, especially his daughter, donate a kidney to save his life. He wouldn't accept the idea. "Yu, I can accept your love, but I won't take your kidney. Removing my daughter's kidney would hurt me more than removing my heart!"

"No!" Han Yu cried, kneeling by the bed. "You've given

me my life. It is nothing to lose one of my kidneys to save your life. I will regret all my life if you don't agree！" Han Yu knelt on the floor and "threatened" her father, "If you don't take my kidney, I will sign a resignation letter to quit my job and kneel down here by your bed day and night..."

Half an hour passed, Two hours passed. Her mother, brothers, and relatives all came to persuade her to get up, but she refused to stand up. There was blood on her knees now and she started to tremble. Her father couldn't bear her hurting herself any more and burst into tears, "My good daughter, just stand up..." Her father nodded to accept the decision.

The hospital was moved by the daughter's love in this nationally unprecedented case. They tried their best to lower the fees. Some pharmaceutical companies offered to give free medicine to her father. An advanced laparoscope was used to take out Han Yu's kidney. They made a small cut in Han Yu's abdomen and took out her kidney with a special tool.

Eighteen years ago, the father gave a life to his little girl. Today, through a ten-minute operation, his daughter helped him regain his life.

(Ah Cheng)

【Comment】

The three children vied with one another to donate their kidneys to save their father's life, and the young daughter knelt down to ask her father to take her kidney. We saw sincere love in her. It is truly moving.

三学子"典身"救娘

　　山东兖州有一户人家，父亲叫尹彦德，母亲叫时苓。他们有 3 个儿子，全都是大学生：大儿子尹训国，中国人民大学法学系硕士研究生；二儿子尹训宁，山东农业大学园艺系学生；三儿子尹训东，山东大学国际贸易系学生。一家出了 3 个大学生，时苓在兖州街头便有了一个响亮的美称："大学生的妈妈"。

　　不幸的是，时苓在抚育孩子期间，患上了乙型肝炎、风湿性关节炎、甲状腺肿瘤等多种疾病。为了孩子们的学习，她一直默默地忍受着病痛的折磨。直到 1999 年突然发起了高烧，血色素降到 1.8 克，生命垂危，不得不躺进济宁医院。经过仔细诊断，她被确诊患有"自身免疫溶血性贫血"。

　　医生说，治疗这种病的惟一办法是置换血浆，每星期至少要换两次，而一次费用就高达 6000 元。尹家父子听后，顿时傻眼了，哪来这么多钱啊。父亲忧愁得来回踱步，三个儿子更是你看看我，我瞅瞅你。最后，他们不得不将自家一套两室一厅带院落的房子以 3 万元的价格卖掉，先解救命之急。

　　3 万元很快便被病魔吞噬了，母亲的病情却依然不见好转。随着病情发展，时苓不得不从济宁医院转至北京友谊医院治疗。

母子情

九九重陽
秋色悲悲
北背娘登高
不言累
娘為兒女
兒背娘
親能苦
絲線回

甲申春月畫
敬老

3个儿子看着一天天消瘦的父亲，再看看生命垂危的母亲，心急如焚。

1999 年 5 月的一天，在北京友谊医院走廊，尹氏三兄弟为筹划医疗费之事苦思冥想。老大尹训国突然眼前一亮，脱口而出："向社会企事业单位求援，提前预领 5 年工资。"老二训宁、老三训东一时茅塞顿开，齐声叫好。兄弟仨就趴在走廊的长椅上，你一句我一句写成了一封《自荐书》:

我们兄弟三人正在读大学，因母亲病重，家中经济困难，急需 5~10 万元。为了挽救母亲，同时为了完成自己的学业，特向有关企事业单位自荐，盼予以接纳。我们将努力学习、提高素质，以优异的成绩回报社会关爱之恩……

1999 年 8 月，《北京晨报》将此消息报道之后，社会上很多好心人被三学子的孝心所感动，纷纷捐款。但是，作为一代有知识的大学生，他们不愿白白接受别人的同情和捐助。他们相信知识的价值和自己的能力。

1999 年 10 月 20 日，陕西汉江药业股份有限公司董事长吕长学和总经理王政军获知山东三学子"典身"救母的消息，被这旷世孝心感动。他俩召集公司西安办事处的同志讨论研究此事，最终达成共识，认为三学子"典身"救母，正符合"把忠心献给祖国、把孝心献给父母、把真诚献给朋友"的企业精神。公司真诚地向学子发出了邀请函。

公司总经理王政军对三学子说："我们接纳你们，一是被你们想尽办法为母亲治病的孝心所打动，这是中华民族的传统美德。二是你们自强自立的创新意识，正是现代企业所需要的。三是面对新世纪知识经济的竞争，企业需要高素质的人才。"王政军最后对三学子语重心长地说，"如果要想挣钱，你们可以选择去南方，如果要想干事，你们可以选择来汉药。"

12 月 25 日，训国三兄弟与陕西汉江药业股份有限公司正式签署了一份特殊的协议，提前领取了 5 年的工资。待毕业之后，他们将无偿为公司工作 5 年。

（文　远洲）

【点评】

知识就是金钱，三学子以预支未来劳动力方式，换取救治母亲的医疗费，体现了现代青年的孝心和价值观。

Three Sons Save Their Mother's Life

There once was a family in Yanzhou of Shandong Province. The father was called Yin Yande and the mother Shi Ling. They had three sons, all university students. The eldest was Yin Xun-guo, a postgraduate studying in the Department of Law at the Renmin (People's) University of China. The second son was Yin Xunning, an undergraduate in the Horticultural Department of Shandong Agricultural University. The third son was Yin Xundong, an undergraduate in the International Trade Department of Shandong University. Shi Ling, who raised three university students, had become famous in her neighborhood and was nicknamed "Mother of University Students."

Unfortunately, during the time she raised the three children, Shi Ling had contracted a number of serious diseases, including hepatitis B, rheumarthritis, and a tumor of the thyroid. She had born all these sufferings for the sake of her children's studies until 1999, when she had a fever and her hemochrome fell to 1.8

grams. She was critically ill and was brought to Jining Hospital, where she was diagnosed with autoimmune hemolytic anemia.

The doctor explained that the only way to treat it was to replace her plasma at least twice a week, costing about 6,000 yuan each time. The whole family was dumbfounded to hear this. Where could they get so much money? The father anxiously paced back and forth and the three sons could do nothing but look at each other. Finally they decided to sell their house, with two bedrooms and one living room, for thirty thousand yuan in order to save their mother's life.

But the money did not last long and the mother's condition did not improve. Shi Ling had to be transferred to the Beijing Friendship Hospital for treatment. Seeing their father getting thinner every day and their mother in danger, the three sons felt their hearts torn with anxiety.

One day in May of 1999, as the sons were standing in the hospital corridor and worrying about the medical fees, Xunguo, the eldest son, suddenly had an idea. "We can ask for support from the community, any company or factory units. We could find a unit that is willing to pay our five years' wages in advance." The other two sons both felt it was a good idea. Then they started to write a self-recommendation letter right on the bench in the corridor.

We three brothers are university students. Our mother is critically ill and our family cannot afford the medical fees. Therefore, we need 50,000 to 100,000 yuan at hand as support. To save our mother's life and finish our studies, we hereby recommend ourselves to any unit that is willing to help us. We will study hard and repay the support of society with good academic scores...

In August of 1999, the Beijing Morning Paper reported the story. Many people were moved by the family's situation and they donated much to help. However, as a generation of university students with education and knowledge, the three sons wouldn't take others' sympathy and charity for nothing. They believed in the value of knowledge and their own abilities.

On October 20, 1999, the Shaanxi Hanjiang Pharmaceutical Co. Ltd. learned about the news. The CEO Lü Changxue and the general manager Wang Zhengjun were moved and called a meeting with the Xi'an Office to discuss the matter. They agreed that the love the three sons showed fit with their enterprise's motto "Show loyalty to the motherland; show love to parents; show sincerity to friends." They sincerely sent out the invitation.

The general manager Wang Zhengjun said to the three sons, "We have decided to accept you not only because we are moved by your filial piety to save your mother's life, which is the traditional virtue of the Chinese nation, but also because you have exhibited the innovative ideas of self-improvement and self-reliance, which is exactly needed in a modern enterprise. We also need talented staff in the modern competition of economy of knowledge." Finally Wang Zhengjun spoke with sincerity to the three students, "If you opt for making more money, you can go to the south. If you opt for doing something real, you can choose Hanjiang Pharmaceutical."

On December 25, the three brothers signed a special agreement with the pharmaceutical plant and had their five years' wages paid in advance.　They agreed to work for five years for the plant after they graduated.

(Yuan Zhou)

【Comment】

Knowledge is money.　The three students raised the money to pay their mother's medical bills by having their future labor paid for in advance—his has demonstrated the modern youth's filial piety and values.

一 餐 之 恩

1992年阳春三月，贵州省兴仁县刚结婚的25岁农村青年余永庄、韦一会夫妇外出打工，在被喻为"煤海"的安龙县龙头大山，不但没有找到工作，反而自身带的1000多元钱被3个歹徒洗劫一空。

夜幕徐徐降下，在空旷的矿山上，听着呼啸的山风，两人感到前所未有的孤独无助，禁不住抱头大哭……

一位正赶牛下山的老人轻轻地拍了拍余永庄的肩膀："娃，哭啥子？"听着这既朴实又厚重、温暖如父爱的声音，余永庄抬起头来，向老人诉说了他们的遭遇。

"我家住在山下，你们可以先到我那里住下。"老人同情地说。余永庄夫妇立即给老人磕头，随着老人下山，来到他的茅屋里。交谈中，余永庄得知老人名叫黄选文，已70多岁了，他老伴名叫李桂兰，小他两岁。李桂兰端出了热气腾腾的晚餐，还专门给他俩各煮了一碗暖身子的荷包蛋。两天一夜没吃上一口东西的余永庄夫妇埋头一阵狼吞虎咽，吃着吃着，泪水落了下来。余永庄握着黄选文的手说："黄伯伯，我一辈子也不会忘记这顿晚餐。"

翌日，黄选文放下手中的农活，带着余永庄夫妇上矿山找工作，有当地人出面，二龙山煤矿收下了他们，余永庄下井采煤，韦一会在井外打杂工。

余永庄夫妇由于忙着打工挣钱，很少下山看望黄选文、李桂兰两位老人。偶尔下山一次，李大娘总是忙前忙后给他们烧水做饭，热情得像久别在外的亲人回家团聚。身处异乡的余永庄夫妇感受到浓浓的人间真情。

1997年12月，打了5年工的余永庄夫妇有了5万多元积蓄，准备返回家乡另谋发展。临行前他们到小镇上买了大包小包的食品来向老人告别，推开门，眼前是一片凄凉的景象：两位老人瘫痪在床，痛苦地呻吟；屋里没有火，缸里没有水，锅里也没有米……黄选文紧紧地拉住余永庄的手，老泪横流……

原来，夫妇两人同时患了脑血栓瘫痪在床。养子黄江此时翻脸不认"爹娘"，将秋收的粮食全部卖掉后，扔下二老带着妻子走了。老人万念俱灰，两次互相抱着滚到门前的堰塘以求一死，都被人及时发现救了起来……

余永庄夫妇赶紧生火烧水给两位老人洗澡、做饭。之后，又跋涉20多公里山路，赶到镇医院给老人开药。

余永庄原打算第二天起程回家，这下却犹豫了。他想，要想缝补老人那颗破碎无望的心，惟一的办法就是尽儿女之孝，使老人安度残年余生。他对妻子说："干脆我们留下来做他们的儿子和媳妇吧？"

"你和我想到一块儿了，我也是放心不下两位老人，他们对我们有恩，我们不能忘恩呀！"

第二天，余永庄让妻子留下照看老人，自己带着这个重大的决定一路直奔兴仁的老家。

回到家，余永庄把自己初上矿山时的情景和眼下黄选文夫妇的境况以及自己的想法向父母说了。父母十分同情黄选文夫妇的遭遇，对余永庄说："孩子，虽然我们把你拉扯长大不容易，我们也老了，也希望你和你媳妇在身边孝敬我们，可黄选文夫妇比我们更苦。俗话说'滴水之恩，涌泉相报'，你的想法是对的，我们支持你。"

余永庄被父母的善良仁义和通情达理深深感动了，他在家里白天拼命地砍柴，手打起血泡仍不肯放下柴刀；晚上给父母洗衣服、搓澡、捶背……离家前他想多做些孝敬父母的事。父母看出了他的心思，催促他说："你快去吧，那边的两位老人还病着呢！"

推开黄选文家的柴门，余永庄拉着妻子来到两位老人的床前，刷地给老人下跪："爸爸、妈妈，以前你们待我们如亲人，现在我们来给你们做儿子、媳妇，为你们养老送终！"老人愣怔了半晌，哆嗦着嘴不知说什么好，两行热泪长流不止……

余永庄夫妇取出5年来打工挣的5万元钱，找来板车将两位老人抱上车，余永庄在前面拉，韦一会在后面推，踏上了一边打工为生、一边四处寻医为老人治病的艰难路。

一晃两年过去了，这期间余永庄夫妇拉着两位老人跑遍了周边的大小医院。又过了半年，在一名老医生的独到治疗和韦一会的精心护理下，两位老人竟都能奇迹般地下地了。

两年之后，两位老人在余永庄夫妇的孝养之下，走完了漫漫人生路，先后离世。送葬那天，余永庄夫妇行孝子之礼，眼里噙着泪，三步一跪，一直跪到巍巍的云盘山极顶……

（文 岑大明）

【点评】

"滴水之恩，涌泉相报"的道理人人都懂，却不是人人都能做到的。余家夫妇的品行，高如云山。

护驹图

初生驴驹
不怕虎
田间陌头迷
归途
急得老
驴啊：
叫
不让
左右离步半

二〇〇三年春天
画护驹图
邢振龄并活

母子情

A Priceless Meal

In March 1992, a young rural couple from Xingren County of Guizhou Province, 25-year-old Yu Yongzhuang and his wife Wei Yihui, left their village to look for jobs after they were married. However, in the Big Dragon Head Mountains of Anlong County, nicknamed the "sea of coal," they couldn't find a single job. What was worse, the 1000 yuan they brought with them was taken by three robbers.

Night fell slowly. Standing on the wide mineral hill and listening to the howling wind, the couple felt lonely and helpless. They burst into tears.

Just then, an old man passed by with his cow. Seeing the couple, he lightly patted Yu Yongzhuang's shoulder, asking, "young man, why are you crying? " Hearing the sincere, father-like, warm voice, Yu Yongzhuang raised his head and told the old man their sad tale.

"I live right at the foot of the hill. You can come and stay with me for now," said the old man sympathetically. The couple knelt down right away and kowtowed. Then they followed the old man to his shed. From their conversation, Yu Yongzhuang learned the old man was Huang Xuanwen, in his seventies, and his wife was Li Guilan, two years younger than her husband.   Li Guilan prepared the couple a good hot meal and cooked two bowls of egg soup especially for them.   Not having eaten anything for two days, the couple immediately started to eat and then began to cry again. Yu Yongzhuang held Huang Xuanwen's hands, saying, "As long as I live, I will never forget this meal."

The second day, Huang put his work aside and took the young couple to look for job on the hill.   With the local man's help, the couple got a job at the Erlongshan Coal Mine. Yu went down the mine well to excavate coal and his wife did some cleaning work there.

As the young couple was very busy, they did not have much time to visit the old couple. Sometimes they would go down the hill to visit them, and they were always treated as if they were the old couple's close relatives. This always brought the warmth to the Yu's.

In December 1997, after five years of work, the Yu couple had over fifty thousand yuan in savings, and they decided to go back home. Before leaving, they went to the town and bought bags of food to say goodbye to the old couple. Pushing the door open, they saw a very sad sight: the old couple was lying in bed, moaning in pain. There was no fire, no water in the pot, no rice in the pan... Huang grasped Yu's hands, tears rolling down his cheeks.

It turned out that both had been struck with cerebral throm-bosis and were paralyzed. Their fostered son Huang Jiang ignored his parents. He sold all the grain and left with his wife, leaving the old couple helpless. Twice the old couple felt hopeless and tried to roll together into the pond to get drown, and were saved by townspeople.

The Yu couple immediately made a fire, cooked a meal, and gave the old couple a bath. Then they traveled mountain road over 20 kilometers to get a prescription from the hospital.

Yu had planned to go home the following day, but what happened made him hesitate. He thought to himself that the only way to mend their broken hearts was to treat them with filial piety and allow them to spend their remaining years in comfort. He said to his wife, "What do you think about staying to be their children? "

"We are thinking alike! We cannot just leave them this way. They have been so kind to us, and we should never forget what the old couple did for us! "

The second day, Yu's wife stayed with the elderly couple and Yu went home to tell his parents about their decision.

At home Yu told his parents all their experiences from the beginning and their thoughts. His parents felt sympathy for the Huang couple and said to their son, "Son, it was not easy for us to bring you up. We are old now too and hoped you two could stay to take care of us. But the Huang couple needs you more than we do. There is a saying: 'Benevolence, even as little as a drop of water, should be returned with a fountain.' You are right and we support you."

Yu Yongzhuang was deeply moved by his parents' kindheartedness and understanding. During the day he cut firewood with all his might, not stopping for even the blisters on his hands. At night he washed clothes for his parents, gave them baths, and massaged their backs. He wanted to do as much as he could for his parents before he set off. His parents could read his thoughts, so they finally urged him to go. "My son, you should go now. The old couple is still ill. They need your help."

Yu pushed Huang's door open, walked up to the bed with his wife, and together they knelt down. "Father and Mother, you treated us like family before, and now I'm your son and she is your daughter-in-law. We are going to look after you forever! "

The old couple was dumb-founded. They were speechless and tears ran down their cheeks.

The young couple took out the fifty thousand yuan that they had saved and found a flat plate cart. They lifted the old couple onto the cart. Yu pulled at the front and Wei pushed at the back. They set off to seek medical treatment for the old couple while doing temporary work on the way.

Two years passed. They went to all the hospitals in the vicinity. Another six months passed, and an old traditional Chinese doctor treated the couple. The treatment and their meticulous care worked wonders. The old couple stood up!

Two years later, both the old man and old woman walked to the end of their life. The young couple followed the traditional rituals. To show their filial piety, they knelt down in tears every few steps on the way to the top of the Yunpan Hill and buried the old couple there.

(Cen Daming)

【Comment】

Everyone knows the truth of "benevolence, even as little as a drop of water, should be returned with a fountain." But not everyone can do as the Yu couple did.

给保姆当保姆

在成都市青羊小区，几乎每天清晨，居民们都会看到71岁的石桂芳大妈用三轮车推着93岁的老奶奶张淑慎散步。张奶奶曾经是石大妈家的保姆，为了报答张奶奶的恩情，石大妈在张奶奶年事已高时义务赡养她，成了张奶奶事实上的保姆。

张淑慎到石桂芳家当保姆始于1964年。在成都，她把石桂芳的两个女儿养大成人，并先后把她们送入了大学校园。为了这俩孩子，张淑慎放弃了自己的婚姻。

滴水之恩，当涌泉相报。对张淑慎老人的默默付出，石家人看在眼里，记在心上，时时寻找着回报的机会。

长大成人的两个女儿石敏与陈玉没有忘记保姆张淑慎的养育之恩。石敏参加工作后挣到的第一笔工资就做了如下的分配：三分之一给保姆张淑慎，三分之一给父母，三分之一留作自己的生活费。她第一次到北京出差，买的惟一一件礼物军用棉鞋，也是给张淑慎的。

1985年5月，张淑慎上街买菜时，不慎脚下一滑，小腿摔成骨折。石桂芳和丈夫陈崇哲将张淑慎送到医院，全家人轮流陪护，喂水喂饭，梳头擦身，尽心尽力，毫无怨言。

1988年夏天，张淑慎的左脚踝部静脉曲张，肿得连鞋都穿不上，本来就行动不便的脚就更加不便行走了。那段时间，石桂芳夫妇真是忙坏了。石桂芳要买菜煮饭，给老人洗澡，为老人护理大小便；每次送老人上医院，陈崇哲都用三轮车接送。

　　1990年，陈崇哲生病去世。临终前，他再三嘱咐家人要谨记张淑慎的恩情，要知恩图报。施惠于人，不要记在心上；受惠于人，则要铭记终身。这是石桂芳一家人的处世哲理。

　　陈崇哲的去世令张淑慎老人伤心不已。在她的心中，她不是石桂芳夫妇的恩人，而石桂芳是她的恩人，是石家给了她一个稳定的生存环境和平等的人格尊严。遭受陈崇哲去世的沉重打击，伤心过度的张淑慎变得沉默寡言，不久得了老年痴呆症，久治不愈。

　　丈夫去世以后，石桂芳又将丈夫肩上的担子一并接了过来。但石桂芳毕竟有一大把年纪了，她开始张罗着给张淑慎找保姆。

　　保姆很快找到了，是一位19岁的小姑娘。保姆来家后，石桂芳特意对保姆进行了严格的"岗前培训"，将张淑慎老人的性格特点、生活习惯、膳食特征等一一向保姆强调说明。当确信新来的保姆可以替代自己时，她才恋恋不舍地从保姆的角色中退了出来。

　　天长日久，了解石家情况的人几乎都被石家人的行为所打动，并受其影响，以尊敬长辈、充满爱心、热爱生活为荣；以忤逆不孝、自私自利、忘恩负义为耻。

（文　文心）

【点评】

　　"施惠于人，不要记在心上；受惠于人，则要铭记终身"。主人为保姆当保姆，这种超越亲情的人际关系值得称道。

A Housemaid for a Housemaid

In the Qingyang Community of Chengdu City, the residents could see 71-year-old Shi Guifang pushing a tricycle with 93-year-old Zhang Shushen sitting in it almost every morning, out for fresh air. Mrs. Zhang used to be a housemaid for Mrs. Shi. In order to return Zhang's meticulous care, Shi promised to take care of Zhang in her advanced age. In fact, she has become a housemaid for Zhang.

Zhang began to serve as a housemaid for Mrs. Shi in 1964. She brought up Shi's two daughters and sent them to universities. For the sake of the two children, Zhang gave up her marriage.

Benevolence, even as little as a drop of water, should be returned with a fountain. The Shi family saw Zhang's devotion to their family and they kept in mind that they would seek opportunities to return her care.

The two children that Zhang brought up, Shi Min and Chen Yu, never forgot their housemaid Zhang's care. After Shi Min graduated from university and got her first month's salary, she decided to give one third to her housemaid Zhang Shushen, one third to her own parents, and the rest to herself. The only gift she bought during her first business trip to Beijing—a pair of cotton-padded military shoes—was for Zhang too.

In May 1985, Zhang slipped and broke her leg when buying vegetables in the bazaar. The Shi couple took her to the hospital and the whole family took turns taking care of her. They fed her, combed her hair, and bathed her. Without complaining, they did all they could to help Zhang.

In the summer of 1988, Zhang's left foot was swollen because of the varicosity in her left ankle. She couldn't wear a shoe, and she could barely walk on her swollen foot. The Shi couple became even busier. Mrs. Shi bought food and cooked, gave Zhang baths, and took care of her. Every time they brought Zhang to the hospital, Chen Chongzhe, Shi's husband, would ride the tricycle to carry Zhang.

In 1990, Chen Chongzhe died of illness. Before he died, he asked the family to remember what Zhang had done for the family. "Do not remember what good you do to others; but never forget what good others do to you." This is the life philosophy for Shi's family.

Zhang was very sad at the death of Shi's husband. She was very grateful to Shi's family, as it was Shi's family that had given her a stable living environment and equal treatment and dignity. The death of Shi's husband was a heavy blow to Zhang. She became very silent. Soon she began to suffer from incurable Alzheimer's disease.

After the death of her husband, Mrs. Shi took over all the family burdens. However, she herself was getting older, so she tried to find a housemaid for Zhang.

She finally found a 19-year-old girl. She gave her some special training and told her about the character and living and eating habits of Mrs. Zhang. Shi didn't quit her role as a house-maid until she made sure the new housemaid could totally replace her and take over.

Time went by. Almost everyone who knew about the Shi family's situation was moved by what the Shi family had done. They took pride in respecting elders, being kindhearted, and loving life, and regarded disobedience to parents, selfishness, and ungratefulness as a disgrace.

(Wen Xin)

【Comment】

Do not remember what good you do to others, but never forget what good others do to you. The example of a master serving as a nurse for her own housemaid is praise-worthy.

一生的痛悔

那一年我从省邮电学校毕业，分配在大别山区一个偏远的小镇上当邮差，我所负责的一条路线是名副其实的穷乡僻壤，邮件少得可怜。这倒好，我总是等它们积攒得差不多了才跑一趟，大概平均半个月一次吧。下面管理松散，也没有人过问。说白了，其实根本没有人注意到一个山村小邮差的存在。只有一位老太太除外。

每逢我送信到她们村，总看见她老远就站在村口。我还没下车，她就迎了上来，小声问："有我儿子的信吗?"

渐渐地，我知道了这位老人的一些事：早年丧夫，惟一的儿子在深圳打工。开始我还在包里翻找一遍，问多了我就有些不耐烦地说："没! 没! 没!"车也不停直奔村长家。

但老人还是不厌其烦地嘱咐我："娃子，有我儿子的信麻烦你给捎来，啊?"

我送信是没有规律的，或10天或半月，但每次总是老远就被老太太迎着。我不知道这位老人是不是每天都这么等着。

有一次真有老人一封信，是从深圳来的。老人拿着信小心翼翼地求我读给她听。我给她念了，又把要紧的解释给她听：“您的儿子春节忙，不回家过年。”

老人的眼里顿时涌出了浑浊的泪。我忙安慰她："但您的儿子很有孝心，马上要给您寄钱和年货回来。"

老人顿时含着泪连连点头，忙不迭地说："唉，唉！多谢娃子，多谢娃子！"

等我将信件送到村长家时，惊奇地看到老人竟比我骑车的先到。只见她高扬着信，神气十足地说："我儿子来信了，要寄钱回来，还寄年货，大城市的年货呢，待过年时到我家尝新鲜！"

村长笑眯眯地说："好嘞！过年我率领全村的男女老少都到你家尝鲜去！"

"好啊，我还得再买些腊鱼腊肉，备足些。我儿子的钱快到了，快到了！"老人因激动而满脸通红。

这一年的冬天似乎特别的寒冷，一场又一场纷飞的大雪将大山、小村和我的心严严实实地覆盖着。我送信的次数越来越少。腊月初八这天，我在旧历年里最后一次来到老人的村庄。老人上前一把拉住我，急切地问："有我儿子的汇款单吗？"

"没有。"我几乎忘了她的儿子曾给她写过那封信也没有在意老人此时的焦虑与不安。一个星期后，我将一些零散的邮件锁进抽屉，提前回家过年了……半月之后回到大别山，我将年前没有送出的邮件整理了一下，准备送出去。突然发现了那位老人的儿子从深圳寄来的汇款单和包裹单，不禁一愣，一种不祥的预兆袭上心头。我马不停蹄地向老人的村庄赶去。可是太迟了，老人已经长眠于村后的坟山上。

据说，老人年前每天都在村口翘首期盼，任凭谁都劝不走。她说："我儿子说到就会做到，除非……除非他出什么事了？"说到这里，老人总是连扇自己几个耳光，然后自我安慰道：

"不会的，不会的，瞧我这乌鸦嘴。我儿子没事的，他会寄来的，我再等等，再等等！"就这样，直到新年的爆竹声响起，村长再一次去劝老人时，发现老人已被冰雪覆盖，成了一尊永远的雕塑。

我手捧汇款单和包裹单跪在老人的坟前痛彻心扉，号啕大哭。

（文　蓝风）

【点评】

因为自己的怠慢和疏忽，酿成了一起人间悲剧。纵使悔痛一生，也唤不回望眼欲穿的那位母亲的生命。让我们像理解和关爱自己的父母一样，去理解和关爱走过我们身边的每一位老人吧！

A Life–Long Regret

After I graduated from the Post & Telecommunications College, I was assigned to work as a postman in a small, remote town in the Dabieshan Mountains. My postal route covered all the poor villages and there were few mailings, so I would make a round only when there was enough mailings, usually once every two weeks. The management was not strict and no one really questioned it. In fact, no one in the mountains even noticed the existence of a postman, except an old grandma.

Every time I passed her village, I saw her standing at the village entrance. She would come up to me before I got off the bike and ask, "Any letter from my son? "

I started to learn a little about this grandma. It turned out that her husband died young and her only son worked as a hired hand in Shenzhen. At first, I would look for the letter in my bag, and after that I got impatient and would always tell her without stopping my bike, "No, no letter from your son."

But the old woman did not mind taking the trouble to urge me again and again, "young man, please do pass me the letter if there is anything from my son."

.   There was really no routine for my delivery; sometimes I would go every ten days or every two weeks.   But every time I would see from far away the old grandma waiting there.   I wondered if she was waiting like that every day.

Once,   there really was a letter from her son from Shenzhen. The old woman held the letter very carefully and asked me to read it for her.   I read it and also explained the important part, "Your son is too busy to come back for the Spring Festival."

Tears suddenly came to her eyes.   I tried to comfort her, "But your son has filial piety.   He is going to send you some money and festival goods."

Hearing this,   the old woman nodded several times with tears in her eyes and said, "Ah, ah. Thank you for telling me that! "

When I rode to the home of the village head,   she had already been there, waving the letter and shouting in a loud voice, "I got a letter from my son.   He is going to send me some money and festival goods, goods from the big city. Come have a taste of the local delicacies! "

The village head smiled and said to the old woman, "Good! On New Year's Eve,   I will bring all villagers to your home to taste the delicacies! "

"Great.   I will buy some more cured fish and meat.   My son's money is coming, coming! " The old woman's face turned red with excitement.

It was very cold that year.   Snow covered all the mountain villages and my heart.   It hampered me from going about my rounds. Finally I made my last round before the traditional Spring Festival. When I came to the village, the old woman came up to me and grabbed me, "Money order from my son? "

"No." I said, almost forgetting that her son had promised to send money and food to his mother. I didn't notice the worry and anxiety on her face either. A week later, I locked the scattered incoming letters in my drawer and returned home early for the traditional Spring Festival. Half a month later, I came back to my office and sorted all the letters that had come in before the holiday. Suddenly I found a money order and a package note. I was surprised and an ominous feeling hit me. I rushed to the old woman's village, only to find that she had already passed away.

I was told that the old woman had waited at the village entrance every day, waiting for the money and food her son had sent to her. No one could persuade her to go back home. She said, "My son would never go back on his word, unless... Is it possible that something happened to him? " Then she would slap her own face and comfort herself, "It can't be. It can't be. My bad mouth. My son will be all right. His money and food will come. I can wait. I can wait! " Day in, day out, she waited there until the New Year's Eve, when there came the sound of firecrackers. When the village head went to see her, intending to ask her to go back home, he discovered that the old woman was already buried in the snow, a permanent sculpture.

With the money order and the package note in my hand, I knelt down before the grave of the old woman, crying.

(Lan Feng)

【Comment】

Dereliction of duty on the part of the postman resulted in a human tragedy. Despite all his regrets, he could never make the old woman live again. Let us understand and care for every elderly person around us just like we understand and care for our own parents.

我和哑巴父亲

  辽宁北部有一个中等城市——铁岭，在铁岭工人街街头，几乎每天清晨或傍晚，你都可以看到一个老头儿推着豆腐车慢慢走着，车上的蓄电池喇叭发出清脆的女孩的声音："卖豆腐，正宗的卤水豆腐！豆腐咧……"

  那声音是我的，那个老头儿，是我的父亲。父亲是个哑巴。直到长到20几岁的今天，我才有勇气把自己的声音放在父亲的豆腐车上，替换下他手里摇了几十年的铜铃铛。

  两三岁时我就懂得了有一个哑巴父亲是多么的屈辱。当我看到有的小孩儿被大人使唤着过来买豆腐，不给钱就跑，父亲伸直脖子也喊不出声的时候，我不会像大哥一样追上那孩子揍两拳，我伤心地看着那情景，不吱一声，我不恨那孩子，只恨父亲是个哑巴。我一直冷冷地拒绝着我的父亲。

  我要好好念书，上大学，离开这个人人都知道我父亲是个哑巴的小村子！这是当时我最大的愿望。

  我终于考上了大学，父亲特地穿上了一件新缝制的蓝褂子，傍晚坐在灯下，表情喜悦而郑重地把一堆还残留着豆腐味儿的钞票放到我手上，嘴里哇啦哇啦地不停地"说"着。我茫然地听着他的热切和骄傲的哇啦声，茫然地看他带着满足的笑容去"通知"亲戚和邻居。当我看到他领着二叔和哥哥们把他精心饲养了两年的大肥猪拉出来宰杀掉，请遍父老乡亲庆贺我上大学的时候，不知道是什么碰到了我坚硬的心弦，我哭了。吃饭的时候，我当着大伙儿的面给父亲夹上几块猪肉，我流着眼泪叫着："爸，爸，您吃肉。"父亲听不到，但他知道了我的意思，眼睛里放出从未有过的光亮，泪水和着高粱酒大口地喝下。

父亲用带着淡淡豆腐味儿的钞票供我读完大学。1996年，我毕业分配回到了距我乡下老家40华里的铁岭。

安顿好一切以后，我去接一直单独生活的父亲来城里享受女儿迟来的亲情。可就在我坐着出租车回乡的途中，我遭遇了车祸。出事后的一切是大嫂告诉我的。

过路的人中有人认出我是老涂家的三丫头，急忙告诉了我的家人。大哥、二哥、大嫂、二嫂先赶来，看着浑身是血不省人事的我哭成一团，乱了阵脚。最后赶来的父亲拨开人群，抱起已被人们断定必死无疑的我，截住路旁一辆大汽车。他用肩扛着我，腾出手来从衣袋里摸出一大把卖豆腐的零钱塞到司机手里，请求司机把我送到医院。嫂子说，从来没见过懦弱的父亲那样坚强而有力量！

在认真清理完伤口之后，医生让我转院，并暗示大哥、二哥准备后事。

父亲扯碎了大哥绝望之际为我买来的寿衣，比划着说："你妹妹不会死的，她才20多岁，她一定行的，我们一定能救活她！"

伟大的父爱，不仅支撑着我的生命，也支撑起医生抢救我的信心和决心。我被推上了手术台。

天地垂怜，我活了下来。但半个月的时间里，我昏迷着，对父亲的爱没有任何感应。面对已成"植物人"的我，人们都已失去信心，只有父亲守在我的床边，坚定地等我醒来！

半个月后的一个清晨，我终于睁开眼睛。我看到一个瘦得脱了形的老头儿，他张大嘴巴，因为看到我醒来而惊喜地哇啦哇啦大声叫着，满头白发很快被汗水濡湿。父亲，我那半个月前还黑着头发的父亲，半个月的时间，好像老了20年！

现在，我除了偶尔的头痛外，看上去十分健康。父亲因此得意不已。我们一起努力还完了欠债，父亲也搬到城里和我一起住了，只是他勤劳了一生，实在闲不下来，我就在附近为他租了一间棚屋做豆腐坊。父亲做的豆腐，香香嫩嫩的，大家都愿意吃。我给他的豆腐车装上蓄电池的喇叭，尽管父亲听不到我清脆的叫卖声，但他一定是知道的，因为每当他按下按钮，他就会昂起头来，露出满脸的幸福和知足。

（文　涂云　黑蝉）

【点评】

伟大的父爱，是生命一盏不灭的灯。

My Deaf Father and I

In the Workers' Street of Tieling City in the northern part of Liaoning province, there is an old man who pushes a small cart, selling bean curd every morning and night. A girl's voice from a loudspeaker in the cart chants for the old man, "Bean curd! My genuine homemade bittern bean curd! Bean curd..."

The voice is mine. The old man is my father. He is a deaf-mute. It is only now, when I have turned 20, that I have had the courage to have my voice recorded and put on my father's cart to replace his old copper bell.

I already felt humiliated to have a deaf and dumb father when I was two or three years old. Sometimes I saw some children, instigated by their parents, come to buy bean curd and then run away without paying. My father could not make a sound. I couldn't catch up with those kids and beat them like my brother did, and I felt very sad. I did not hate these children. I hated my father for being mute. So I always turned a cold shoulder to my father.

I knew I had to study hard and go to a university so as to

bid farewell to this small village where everybody knew that my father was a mute. That was my greatest wish at that time.

I finally entered a university. My father put on his new clothes and in the evening, he joyfully put the money that he earned, still smelling of bean curd, into my pocket and made some sounds like he was talking to me. He was full of enthusiasm and pride. I listened to him without any feelings and saw him go to "tell" relatives and neighbors the news with excitement. When I saw him leading my uncle and brothers to kill a big pig that he had raised for two years, and inviting the whole village to celebrate my university enrollment, I felt something hit my hard heart. I cried. During the meal I put some pieces of meat into my father's bowl in front of everyone and said with tears in my eyes, "Dad, Dad. Have some meat." My father couldn't hear it, but he knew what I meant. His eyes were bright and he drank his glass of wine mixed with his tears.

My father paid my tuition all the way to graduation with his bean curd money. In 1996, I graduated and was assigned to work in Tieling, about twenty miles from my village.

When I settled down, I planned to go back home to take my father to the city so he could enjoy himself. Unfortunately, a traffic accident occurred on my way home in a taxi. My aunt told me what happened.

Some passersby recognized me and told the bad news to my father. My two brothers and their wives arrived at the scene first. Seeing me bleeding and unconscious, they started crying together. My father rushed to the site last, picked me up, and stopped a

中华敬老故事精选

Selected China Stories of Elder—Respecting

truck. Carrying me on his shoulder, he took out some money and put it into the driver's hand, asking him to take me to a hospital. My aunt told me that she had never seen my weak father so full of strength.

After cleaning my wounds carefully, the doctor suggested transferring me to another hospital and hinted to my brothers to prepare for my funeral.

In despair my father tore to pieces the grave clothes my brother bought and gestured, "Your sister won't die. She is only in her twenties. She will make it. We can bring her back! "

My father's great love not only supported my life but also gave confidence to the doctors. I was taken into the operation room.

It turned out that I did not die. But during the two weeks' time, I was in a coma, with no feeling of my father's love. Seeing me as a vegetable, people around almost lost their confidence, but my father, who stayed by my bedside, firmly believed that I would wake up.

Half a month later, I opened my eyes one morning at last. I saw a thin old man with his mouth wide open, shouting in surprise and excitement, with his gray hair full of sweat. My father, whose hair was black just two weeks ago, had aged twenty years in only two weeks!

Now I am quite well except for some occasional headaches. My father is delighted. We worked together and paid all the debts back. My father moved to Tieling City and stays with me. As he is not comfortable staying at home doing nothing, I rent a small room in the neighborhood so he can continue to make bean curd, which is very tender and delicious and has become very popular. I bought a loudspeaker and had my voice recorded, imitating a vendor. Although my father can't hear it, when he pushes the button, he holds his head high, his face brimming with happiness and satisfaction.

(Tu Yun, Hei Chan)

【Comment】

Great fatherly love is a lamp of life that will never go out.

俺 爹 俺 娘

1998年岁末的北京，被一段人间真情感动着。一个儿子，20年如一日，把镜头对准生他养他的爹娘，纪录下这对相濡以沫大半个世纪的老夫老妻的情感历程。从这些照片中挑选出来的精华《俺爹俺娘》组照，在首届中国国际民俗摄影大赛中获得了最高奖——"人类贡献奖"。12月1日，《俺爹俺娘》专题摄影个人展在中国美术馆开展，剪彩的不是领导、名人，而是孝子专程从山东鲁中山区请来的84岁的爹和86岁的娘。这一天，正是娘86岁生日，也是爹娘结婚68周年。

这个儿子，就是《人民日报》（海外版）摄影记者焦波。

看着为爹娘拍的一叠叠照片，焦波心中很是欣慰。他要为大半辈子从没照过相的爹娘积累厚厚的几大本影集，给儿孙们留下点想头。于是，为爹娘摄影成了焦波生活中不可或缺的内容。

他拍爹娘在生活了几十年的农家小院里的日常起居；拍爹娘周围的风土人情；拍爹娘逛北京、手拉手登长城；拍爹娘爬泰山进香还愿；拍娘给爹挠痒痒；拍爹给娘剪小脚指甲；甚至拍爹和娘吵嘴生气……

舔犢圖

人間親情
有幾分
骨肉見親情
親又親
桃花潭水
左情好
相濡以沫
愛情真
直舐犢圖
二〇〇三年春天
邢振齡並詩

母子情

焦波的爹娘闹不清，儿子为啥总对着"长得不好看"的爹娘拍来拍去。但他们明白，也只有儿子才会这样做，爹娘对儿子是无私的，儿子对爹娘也是无私的。

焦波说，爹娘没有文化，却教给了他做人的道理；爹娘清苦一世，却给了他一生受用不尽的财富。每次回家，除了给爹娘摄影，剩下的时间他都跟爹娘聊天，他知道80多岁的爹娘不会有太多的时间了。跟爹娘团聚的机会总是很少，焦波一人在外闯天下，积蓄不多，但他还是拿出几千元钱给住在山村里的爹娘安了部电话，以便天天能听到爹娘的声音，向爹娘问候一声。

从前年开始，娘的身体状况每况愈下，按照农村的观念，人过80就该等死了，有了病也不去治。焦波千叮咛万嘱咐："我不在家，爹娘有啥病，一定要及时去治，去最好的医院，请最好的大夫，用最好的药，花多少钱你们不用操心。"经过精心治疗调理，娘的病大见好转，乡邻们都说："焦波硬是用钱买回了他娘的命啊！"焦波说："钱花了咱可以再挣，亲娘可是只有一个呀！"

他想让爹娘在有生之年多看看美好的大千世界，把爹娘接到北京，搀着二老逛了故宫，登上了长城，了却了爹娘多年的心愿。在故宫，焦波激动地把娘抱了起来，说："娘，您抱了俺一辈子啦，俺也抱抱您吧！"妻子抢拍下这个镜头。"在北京我抱了抱娘，在泰山我量了量娘，在家里我称了称娘，心里很难受。娘只有1米41，才70斤重，这就是生了我们兄弟姐妹8个，养大了我们4个的娘吗？她的生命都快熬干了！"

焦波感慨地说："我要一直拍下去，直拍到爹娘离开人世，然后把爹娘一辈子的照片整理出版一部画册。"这是一个儿子对爹娘最真挚的回报。

（文　施晓亮）

【点评】

坚持不懈20年，摄下父母真实、质朴的情感。所赢得的，不仅是一个摄影大奖，更是人们对孝子的一份敬重。

My Father and Mother

A moving story spread in Beijing toward the end of 1998. A son recorded with his camera the life story of his father and mother over a period of twenty years. The carefully chosen series of photos called "My Father and Mother" won the highest prize for Human Contribution in the first Chinese International Folk Custom Photography Competition. On December 1, My Father and Mother, a personal photography exhibition, was exhibited in the China Gallery. The people who cut the ribbon at the grand opening weren't any leaders or famous people, but the old couple themselves, the 84–year–old father and 86–year–old mother, specially invited by their son from the Luzhong mountain area of Shandong Province. The opening day was the 86th birthday of the mother and the 68th anniversary of the marriage of the old couple.

The son was Jiao Bo, a photographer for the People's Daily (Overseas Edition).

Seeing the pictures of his father and mother, Jiao Bo felt very gratified. He had wanted to make several thick photo albums for his father and mother, who had never had their pictures taken in their whole life. He wanted his parents to leave some images for their children and grandchildren. Therefore, taking pictures of his parents became part of his life.

He started photographing his parents in their daily life in a small farm courtyard in which they had lived for years. He recorded with his camera their neighbors and the local customs and conventions; he had happy shots of his parents seeing sights in Beijing and ascending the Great Wall hand in hand; he recorded how his parents burnt incense and prayed for a happy life at Mount Tai; and he also recorded how his mother scratched itches for his father and how his father cut his mother's toenails, and even scenes of the old couple quarreling.

Jiao Bo's parents didn't know why their son enjoyed taking pictures of them, because they never thought they were good-looking. But they could understand only their son could do so because they and their son were selfless to each other.

Jiao Bo said that his parents didn't know how to read and write, but they taught him how to be a good man; they had lived a very simple and hard life, but they had given him an inexhaustible wealth. Every time he went back home, he chatted with his parents and took pictures, as he knew his old parents didn't have much time left in their lives. Although he did not have many chances to stay with his parents and did not have much money, since he was living and working on his own, he had a telephone installed for his parents so that he could hear their voices every day.

The year before last, Jiao Bo's mother fell ill and became

worse and worse. It was the traditional village idea that if one passes 80, he should just wait for death without taking any medicine. Jiao Bo told his parents again and again, "Since I am not at home, if you get ill, you must immediately go to the best hospital, see the best doctors, and take the best medicine. Don't worry about the money." Under meticulous care, his mother became much better. Their neighbors all said, "It was Jiao Bo who saved his mother's life with his money." Jiao Bo responded, "I can always earn more money after I use it up, but I have only one mother! "

Jiao wanted his parents to see more of the good sights of the country in their remaining years. He took his parents to Beijing and accompanied them to tour the Forbidden City and the Great Wall. In the Forbidden City, he clasped his mother with excitement and said, "Mom, you have held me all my life, now you deserve it too! " His wife recorded the scene. "In Beijing I embraced my mom. At Mount Tai I measured my mom's height. At home I weighed my mom. I feel sad. My mom is only 141 cm tall and weighs only 35 kilograms. Is this our mom who gave birth to us eight children and brought up four of us? We have almost dried up her life! "

"I will continue to take pictures of my parents until they pass away, and I will publish an album about their whole life, " Jiao said, adding that this is his sincerest return for what his parents have done for him.

(Shi Xiaoliang)

【Comment】

Jiao persisted for twenty years in taking photos of his parents, recording their true and simple feelings. What he has won is not only a grand prize, but the highest respect for his love for his parents.

给父亲搓澡

　　我与父母同住一座城市。忙完工作后猛然想起，该去看看两位老人了。

　　乘车回到家，二老特别高兴，尤其是父亲，又是沏茶又是洗水果，仿佛来了什么贵客。坐着闲聊了一会儿，父亲像是想起什么，对我说："繁杰，下面那条街新开了个澡塘子，挺好的。我要去洗个澡，你不一块儿去泡泡？"

　　新开张的浴池顾客不多。坐在热水池边，蒸腾的热浪，朦胧的雾气，极易撩拨起人遥远的遐思……未与父亲一同洗澡，怕有40个年头了。依稀记得，那时父亲特别爱进澡塘，每次去都要拽上我。记忆中的父亲壮极了，每当脱去衣服步入浴室，他就逼我下热水池。见我努着嘴往后缩，他便自己跳进池中，一边念叨着"不烫不烫，你看我……"一边趁我不注意冷不丁将我抱起，不由分说摁入水中……泡上一阵后，他又开始了第二道工序：为我搓澡。父亲坐在池边，将我放在腿上，或趴或仰，然后将毛巾拧干绕在手掌上。父亲的手很有力，又格外仔细，由脸颊、脖颈顺着前胸后背次第搓起，手掌过处非痛即痒，任我嚷着："别搓了，爸爸，干净啦……"父亲却依然故我，像是在耐心地打磨擦拭着一件珍贵的祖传器皿：先整体，后局部，直至耳根、双腋、脚丫缝儿……

上小学后不久，我考入了省艺校，至此离开了父母的怀抱。如今我已年近半百，父亲长我三旬，已垂垂老矣。在更衣间，随着父亲衣裳的一件件剥落，我做儿子的心一阵阵紧缩，我做梦也不会想到，失去衣物遮饰的父亲会如此苍老：前腹凹陷，后脊如弓，根根肋骨清晰可辨，失去光泽的皮肤枯树皮般布满皱褶和黑褐色的斑点……我的鼻子阵阵发酸，突然想起半年前母亲曾讲过，父亲一改爱烫澡的多年老习惯，不愿进澡塘了。对此，我曾大惑不解，今天谜底解开：父亲早已不似当年，他已近耄耋之龄，一人进澡塘，很容易发生意外。或许他曾因浴室太滑而摔倒；或许他曾因池塘太热而昏厥……只是尚未出大问题，怕家人担心，怕牵累儿女，便紧缄其口，然而却再也不愿独自迈进浴池之门……

父亲浸在热水池中，惬意地哼着小曲。见父亲泡得差不多了，我将他搀出池塘，该开始搓澡了。虽然身旁就有热情揽客的搓澡工，我还是决定亲自动手，就像当年父亲为我搓澡那样，为他老人家仔仔细细、认认真真地搓搓澡。因为我清楚，我们父子俩这种肌肤相亲的时日是非常有限的，说不定哪一天，我会永远失去这种机会。我将父亲搀扶到搓澡床上，学着当年父亲的样儿，将毛巾缠于手掌，从脸颊、脖颈顺着前胸后背次第搓起……父亲静静地躺着，双眼微眯，孩子似的任我摆布，喉咙中时不时嘟噜出一句："真舒服……"

哦，父亲，请原谅您儿子的疏忽。从今往后，儿子不管多忙，都会抽空来看您，陪您老人家进澡塘，给您老人家搓澡。

（文　孟繁杰）

【点评】

为年迈的父母搓澡，就像父母为小时候的我们洗澡，是爱心，也是天经地义的责任。

A Rubdown for My Father

My parents and I live in the same city. After I finished work one day, an idea suddenly crept into my mind that I would like to see my parents.

My parents were very happy to see me back, especially my father. He made tea and prepared fruit, as if I were a distinguished guest. Chatting for a while, my father suddenly thought of something and said to me, "Fanjie, there is a new bathhouse open, a good one. I am going for a bath. Are you coming with me? "

There were not so many people there. We sat on the pool side, wave upon wave of hot water and the mists stirring my thoughts. It might have been forty years since we bathed together. At that time, whenever my father went to the bath, he would take me along. When we came to the bathing room, he would tell me to get into the hot pool. Seeing me stepping back, he would get into the pool himself and say to me, "It's not hot. Not at all. You see, I am fine..." Then he would grab me and press me into the hot water. A moment later, he started his second step on me: giving me a rubdown. He sat by the pool and wrapped the towel around his hand, me on his lap either on my stomach or on my back. My father had a strong hand and he was also very careful. He would start at my cheeks and neck, and then move from my chest to my back. Because of his strong hand, it was itchy and painful and I would shout, "Stop, Dad! I am clean enough! " But my father didn't stop. Instead, he kept going patiently as if he was rubbing a precious antique passed down for generations: first the whole body, then different parts, behind the ears, under the arms and between the toes...

After a few years in primary school, I entered an art school in the province and left my parents. Now I had almost turned 50, and my father was 30 years older than me. In the locker room, my father started to take off his clothes and I felt my heart shrinking. I could never imagine what I saw: my father appeared so old. He was hunched over from old age and I could see his ribs. His skin was like dry bark, full of wrinkles and black spots. I felt sad and suddenly I remembered that my mother told me half a year ago that my father had changed his habit and stopped going to the bathhouse. I was very confused at that time, but now I saw the reason. My father was no longer what he used to be. Anything could happen to him in the bathhouse when he was very old. Perhaps he slipped once and fell, or perhaps fainted because of the heat. Therefore, he kept his mouth shut because he didn't want to bring worry and trouble to his family. He was not willing to go to the bathhouse by himself any more.

My father sat in the water, singing a small tune. After a

while, I helped him out of the pool into a bed and began to rub his back very carefully, just like what he did for me when I was young, even though there was a professional employee doing a better job. I knew we wouldn't have many opportunities to be together like this and someday I would lose the chance forever. I started to follow what my father did to me. I wrapped the towel around my hand and started to rub my father from his cheeks and neck to his chest and back. My father lay there quietly; his eyes forming a line, and from time to time murmured, "It feels so good."

Oh, Father, I beg your forgiveness for my negligence. From now on I promise to take time out to see you often, no matter how busy I am, and will take you to the bathhouse and give you a nice rubdown.

(Meng Fanjie)

【Comment】

It is love and also duty to give a rubdown to our parents just like they did for children when they were young.

给 娘 洗 脚

　　32年前，我从山西晋南农村入伍，从此走进城市。但每逢年节，只要时间允许，我都要回家看看老娘。

　　近年由于工作离不开，未能实现这一约定。今年除夕的上午，我在车站等待搭乘回乡的班车。天上飘着大雪，耳边鞭炮声此起彼伏，时隔两年没见到老娘了，班车徐徐进站，我的眼泪扑簌簌地往下落。

　　那天晚上，屋外仍然飘着雪花。我陪娘说着话，也悄悄烧好了洗脚水。第一次给娘洗脚是1958年的秋天，我只有8岁。那时国家正处于"大跃进"时期，男人和青壮劳力都外派大炼钢铁了，生产队里只留下老弱妇幼坚持农业生产。有一天，队里安排娘和几个老太太起牛圈粪，这种活在农村是重体力劳动，但没有青壮劳力，老太太也要"革命加拼命"。和娘一块起牛圈粪的都是从旧社会走过来的小脚女人，尖尖的鞋子一踩进粪泥里就拔不出来，老太太们不得不临时回家缝钉鞋带。一尺多厚的牛粪在牛蹄子的踩压下非常坚硬，老太太们用镢头挖吧，镢头太重，抡不起来；用铁锹挖吧，脚小无力踩不下去。

　　娘和几位老姐妹们硬是用蚂蚁啃骨头的精神，挖一点就用簸箕端出去，整整一个上午，5间房大的牛圈粪刚起出三分之一。

中午饭时，娘一手端着从生产队食堂领回家的4个糠菜团子，一手拉着妹妹的手说："咱娘俩少吃点儿，叫你二哥和三哥多吃几口。他们念书费脑子，将来要干大事。要饿就先饿咱娘俩，实在太饿了咱吃榆树叶。"说着娘把一个糠菜团子掰成两半，递给妹妹半个，自己吃半个，剩下的3个看着我和哥哥一口一口地吃下去。

那天晚上，娘累散了架，连鞋都没脱就倒在炕上睡着了。二哥那时住校，我做完作业上炕时，发现炕沿上娘那双沾满牛粪的鞋，萌发了为娘脱鞋洗洗脚，让娘睡个好觉的想法。当我解开鞋带脱掉粪鞋又脱袜子的时候，无论如何也脱不下来。原来，娘的袜子和脚已经被血粘在一起了。我只好叫醒娘，让她将小脚慢慢地伸进洗脚盆，浸了好一会儿，我才轻轻地给她把湿漉漉血淋淋的袜子脱下来。娘那被缠脚带缠变了形、蜷曲在脚掌下的4个脚趾全被铁锨顶烂了。我一边小心翼翼地给娘洗脚，一边对娘说："娘，明天不要去队里上工了。"娘抚摸着我的脑袋说："庄稼人，哪有那么娇气？不干活挣工分，你们吃什么？"我流着泪看着娘不说话，娘一边为我擦泪一边说："娘没事，睡吧，明天还要上学哩！"

岁月悠悠，往事仍历历在目。我捧着老娘现在已经瘦得皮包着骨头的双脚，真让人难以相信它能够支撑同样瘦弱的身体。但正是这双脚，曾经奔波在田间地头和沟壑小路，支撑起家庭重负，为我们创造幸福。我用从天津买回来的专用修脚工具为娘剪去脚指甲又磨光棱痕，还小心翼翼地扳开卷曲的脚趾缝，抠出污垢。今年除夕夜，50岁的人能为88岁的老娘洗脚，我深情地感到是生活对儿子的恩赐！能为老娘尽点孝心，是人生最大的快乐和享受。

　　如果有可能，我愿年年回家守候爱我、惦记我的老娘，为她洗脚、修脚。

（文　张有德）

【点评】

　　一家大公司招聘工作人员时，主管要问一句："你给母亲洗过脚吗？"得到肯定回答者一般会考虑录用。这个企业是把善待父母尊敬长者和敬业精神联系起来了。细想一下是有道理的，一个连父母都不善待的人，能善待他人、勤勉敬业吗？

Washing My Mother's Feet

Thirty–two years ago, I joined the army in my village in the south of Shanxi Province, and I stationed in a city. Whenever I had time, I would return home to see my mother.

In recent years, however, I had been too busy to act as I had promised. On the morning of New Year's Eve, I stood at a train station waiting for the train to go back home. It was snowing heavily and there came the sound of firecrackers now and then. Having not seen my mother for two years, I started to cry as the train approached the station.

That evening, it was still snowing outside. Inside I talked with my mother and prepared some warm water. I washed my mother's feet for the first time since 1958, when I was eight years old. It was the time of Great Leap Forward. All the strong men and laborers were sent out for steel production and only old people, children, and women stayed to work in the farm fields. One day, my mother and other old women were asked to dig the cow dung, which was considered to be some heavy work in the village. Without strong laborers, the old women had to do it themselves, as a kind of contribution to the revolution. The old women my mother worked with had bound feet, which were considered to be beautiful in old society. It was very hard for the old women to pull out their small, sharp shoes when they stepped into the dung. So they had to go back home to sew their shoelaces tight. The cow dung, more than thirteen inches thick, was very hard for the old women. They tried to use the hoe, but it was too heavy for them. They tried the shovel, but it was too hard for their tiny feet.

My mother and other old women worked very hard to dig out the dung little by little with dustpans. Working one whole morning, they dug out one third of the dung, the size of five big rooms.

At lunch, my mother brought the four bran balls from the canteen and said to my younger sister, "We two must eat less so that your two brothers can have more. They study hard so they need more food. We can eat some elm leaves if we are really hungry." Then she split one bran ball into halves and gave my sister half. She watched the two of us finish the other three balls.

That night my mother was so tired that she fell asleep with her shoes on. At that time, my elder brother lived at the school. When I finished my homework and saw my mother's shoes with the dung all over, the idea crept into my mind that I must wash her feet so that she could have a sound sleep. When I was taking off her shoes, I found that her feet were stained with blood and the socks were stuck to her feet. I had to wake up my mother and put her small feet into the water. After a while I gently took off her blood-stained socks. My mother's contorted bound feet were a mess because of the shovel. I washed them carefully and said to my mother, "Mom, don't go to work tomorrow." My mother caressed my head and said, "We are peasants, who never get spoiled. What will we eat if we don't work?" I just looked at my mom without saying anything, tears in my eyes. My mother wiped my tears and continued, "I am fine. You need to go to bed now. You still have to go to school tomorrow."

Now years have passed, but the old days still seem fresh. Looking at her skinny feet, I could hardly imagine that they could support her equally thin body. But it was these very feet that took her to the fields and down the mountain roads; it was these feet that supported the heavy burdens of the family and brought happiness for us. I used the pedicure tools I bought from the city to carefully trim her nails and clean her feet. Tonight, on the eve of the New Year, I felt the grace life had given to me as I, a man that has turned 50, was still able to wash my 88-year-old mother's feet. To be able to show my love to my mother like this was the greatest happiness and enjoyment I could ever have.

If possible, I will go home every year to be with my mother, who has been loving and missing her son. I will wash and pedicure her feet.

(Zhang Youde)

【Comment】

When a big company was recruiting employees, the manager asked the question, "Have you ever washed your mother's feet?" If the employee had, he was likely to be recruited. The company associated those who hold their parents in high esteem with the spirit of loyalty to their profession. There is something in it. It would be hard to imagine that a person who is not kind to his parents can be kind to others and committed to his or her profession.

奶奶的大爱

　　73岁的徐月兰，原来有一个温馨的家。后来因为一次事故，一家五口人只剩下了她和孙女刘敏。刘敏天资聪颖，考上了大学。但是面对卧病在床的奶奶，她只能放弃继续上学的机会。徐月兰把孙女叫到床前说："孩子，自古以来哪有中了状元放弃的？"刘敏哭着问："奶奶，我走了你怎么办？""奶奶我有百岁命，死不了的。想起我有个上大学的好孙女，我的病一下就好了！"徐月兰回答。

　　徐月兰卖掉了家里所有值钱的东西，乡邻们又帮着凑了一些钱，打点刘敏上大学去了。

　　徐月兰则打起包袱到县城当了保姆。尽管她干活特别卖力，但毕竟年老手脚不灵活，结果半年不到换过4个主人。

　　在走投无路之际，徐月兰想到了乞讨。

　　从开始乞讨的第一天，徐月兰就意识到从此以后的一切行动都必须对孙女保密。为了防止碰上熟人，她常在头上扣顶帽子或缠条布帕。

　　徐月兰把讨来的零钱换成大钞，每月一次地从邮局汇往兰州。如果是300元以内，她谎称是给人家当保姆挣的工资；如上了400元，就谎称某某亲戚朋友送了100元；如果凑够500元以上，她则谎称又向谁借了钱。总之不能让孙女生疑。

那年暑假，刘敏要回家探望祖母。徐月兰慌了手脚，她把讨饭行头寄存了，又到理发店染了头发，痛痛快快洗个澡，换上了干净衣服。

刘敏回来后见奶奶蛮有精神的，很是高兴。

等孙女一走，徐月兰又踏上了去省城的行乞之路……

一个血色黄昏，徐月兰因心脏病发作，倒毙路旁。

一根青色的竹棍，一只深蓝色布袋，一个盛着1元9角钱的瓷碗。抚摸着奶奶留下的三件遗物，撕心裂胆的刘敏只喊了一声"奶奶啊"便晕倒过去……

刘敏的成绩在全校名列前茅。她珍藏着奶奶的三件遗物，默默起誓：奶奶，您安息吧，您的大恩，托起的将是一轮太阳！

（文 梵宫）

【点评】

大像无形，大音稀声，大爱无言。奶奶的大爱，尽在不言之中。人间的至情至爱，大都如此，做儿女的都要细心体会才是。

The Great Love
of My Granny

73-year-old Xu Yuelan used to have a warm family. But an accident broke her family, leaving only herself and her grand-daughter Liu Min. Although Liu Min had passed the university entrance examination with her talents, she had to give up the chance to continue her education to take care of her bedridden granny. Xu called her granddaughter to the bedside, saying, "My child, it is not reasonable for you to give up your chance." Liu Min cried and asked, "But Granny, who will take care of you if I go to college?" "I can live up to 100 years," Xu an-swered. "When I think of my good granddaughter in a universi-ty, my illness will just go away."

Xu sold all the family's valuables and neighbors also con-tributed, and finally her granddaughter went to college.

Xu found a job as a housemaid in the county town. But she was too old and her jobs never lasted long. Within half a year, she lost her job four times, even though she worked very hard.

Seeing no way out, she thought of begging.

From the very first day of her begging, she decided that she would keep it secret to her granddaughter. She would put on a big cap or wrap up her head so that acquaintances would not recognize her.

Every month, she would change the small money she got from begging into bank notes and send them to her granddaughter in Lanzhou. If it was within 300 yuan, she would tell her granddaughter it was her salary as a housemaid. If it was around 400 yuan, she would say that she got the extra 100 yuan from some of her relatives or friends. If it was more than 500 yuan, she would say that she borrowed it. She would say anything to keep her granddaughter from suspecting.

That summer vacation, Liu Min decided to return home to see her granny, throwing Xu into a panic. She hid all her begging things, had her hair dyed, took a bath, and put on clean clothes.

Liu came back and was very happy to see everything was fine with her granny.

As soon as Liu returned to school, Xu went to town to beg again. But as dusk fell one day, Xu was struck by a heart attack and died by the roadside.

Seeing the three things left by her granny, a green bamboo stick, a dark blue cloth bag, and a porcelain bowl with 1 yuan and 90 cents in it, Liu Min was sorely grieved. Crying out "My granny!" she fainted.

Liu Min came out among the best in her university. She

cherished the three things her granny left and took an oath: May your soul rest in peace, granny. Your great love will lift a star!

(Fan Gong)

【Comment】

The great love of the granny lies in her silence, as does all the fervent love in the world. It requires careful learning from experiences for those sons and daughters.

为母当红娘

我永远记得1980年那个夏天，父母为了把家里仅有的两间草房改为瓦房，没日没夜地苦干，结果父亲积劳成疾，不幸溘然去世。母亲望着高高矮矮的4个孩子，哭得昏天黑地，死去活来。

那时，才42岁的母亲，多想再找一个伴侣共同支撑风雨飘摇的家呀！然而，"好女不嫁二夫"的世俗偏见，像把利剑悬在母亲头上，使她不敢越雷池半步。她只好用自己的勤劳智慧，在苦日子里打拼。终于，家里的境况发生了变化，我们四兄妹先后考上大学，参加工作进了城。幸福，正一天天向母亲靠近，她整日乐呵呵的。

前年，我回乡下把年过花甲的母亲接到城里居住。城里冰冷的防盗门阻隔了人与人之间的交际往来，她整天只身一人呆在房中，盯着父亲20年前的遗像发愣。

我和妻分析原因，商讨对策。妻说："爸去世多年，妈没了伴儿，少是夫妻老是伴，为使妈摆脱寂寞，还是找个后爸好。"我一听陡然开窍：我们居委会不是有支秧歌队吗？母亲跳秧歌舞在乡下十里八村是有口皆碑的。对，就让她先加入秧歌队！

婆媳圖

都說骨肉心相連
孝男順女親無間
請君賞我此畫圖
卻是婆媳勝血緣

甲申年春天畫詠老故事

邢振齡畫並題

秧歌队的队长就是住在我们隔壁单元的胡叔。前几年胡婶病逝了，两个儿子都在外地工作，留下他一人独守空房。自从母亲加入秧歌队后，胡叔每天都来约她去跳舞，母亲也毫不推辞。渐渐地，我和妻发现，母亲越来越注重形象了。每次跳舞之前都要描眉、涂口红、打摩丝……跳舞结束后，胡叔总是把她送到家门口。两位老人呆在一起的时候，有说有笑，幸福洋溢在脸上。

两个月后的一天，母亲身体不适没去跳舞。胡叔得知后，竟提着一副中药上我家来了。妻子当着两位老人的面，趁机说："妈、叔，你们别瞒着我们了，结婚吧！"也许是妻子这话说得太突然，两位老人的脸上泛起了红晕。母亲说："我们想过这事……"胡叔在一旁补充道："只怕你们反对！""哪能呢？你们辛辛苦苦把儿女养大，现在过上了好日子，理所当然应找个伴。"我回答。

重阳节那天，阳光灿烂。我和妻陪着两位老人来到民政部门办理结婚证。民政助理员问："你们是自由恋爱吗？""是。"两位老人异口同声答道。"红娘是谁？""儿子和媳妇。"办公室里的人发出一阵啧啧称赞声。我和妻会心地笑了。

（文　牟伦祥）

【点评】

为母亲当红娘，是社会文明和进步的表现。敬老不仅表现为物质上的供养，更需要尊重老人生活方式的选择，满足老人情感上的需要。

A Go–Between for Mother

I will never forget the summer of 1980. In order to remodel our home's only two huts into a tile–roofed house, my father overworked himself day and night and finally broke down from the constant strain. Soon he passed away. Looking at their four children of different ages, my mother cried her heart out.

My mother was then only 42. She could easily find a companion to help her support the family. But the old idea that a good wife doesn't marry again dies hard, and she refused to overstep the old conventions. She worked very hard in those days and the family situation started to get better. She paid the tuition for all four sisters and brothers through college until we graduated and found jobs. Felicity was approaching gradually and she was very happy every day.

The year before last, I took my mother to the city. But in the city, the ice–cold burglarproof door separated people. She was all alone at home and could only look at the portrait of her deceased husband, who died twenty years ago.

My wife and I sat together and had a talk about it. My wife

said, "Your father's death left your mother very lonely. In order to help mother get rid of loneliness, it might be good to find her a companion." I thought about it and an idea came into my mind: there is a dance team in the neighborhood that does the yangko dance, a popular rural folk dance. My mother excels at it. Why not just ask her to join the dance team?

Uncle Hu, the team leader, lived right next door to our apartment. His wife passed away a few years ago and his two sons both worked out of the city, leaving him alone. Since my mother joined the dance team, he invited my mother to dance every day and my mother never refused. By and by, my wife and I found that my mother paid more attention to her appearance and would put on makeup before going to dance. Hu always took her back home. The elderly couple was very happy when they were together.

Two months later, feeling ill, my mother didn't go to dance one day. Hu brought some medicine for my mother. Seizing this chance, my wife proposed right in front of them, "Mom, Uncle! Don't be shy with us. We totally support your marriage!" What my wife said brought a blush into these old people's cheeks. My mother said, "We actually thought about this." "And we were afraid that you two wouldn't agree," Hu added. I answered, "We wouldn't say no. It was not easy for you to bring up your children in the old days, and now we all live a good life. You need to have a companion."

On the Double Ninth Festival, a Chinese traditional festival, we accompanied the old couple to the Civil Affairs Bureau to get a marriage license. The assistant asked, "Is this your own choice to get married? " "Yes, " the couple answered together. "Who is your go-between? " "My son and his wife." We received much praise from the people in the office and we smiled.

(Mou Lunxiang)

【Comment】

To act as a go-between for a mother is a demonstration of social progress. Respect for elders is expressed not only in material support but also, and more important, in the respect for their choice of way of life so as to satisfy their emotional needs.

我为母亲擀寿面

　　从小时候起，我最爱吃的就是母亲的手擀面。那面条，细细长长的，吃到嘴里，凝脂般滑润；嚼起来，"格登登"的特有"咬劲"。调上点炸酱，满口生香，但因家境贫寒，这样的美食很少有机会品尝。好在邻里百家偶有盖房、办喜事的，常请母亲去擀面，母亲便会捎一碗人家送的面条，让我解馋。

　　我参加工作后便离开母亲到了外地。每次回家，母亲总要亲自为我擀面条。民间俗语："进门饺子，出门面"。说的是用又细又长的面条牵住亲人的心。看着她佝偻着身躯，吃力地推动着擀面杖，稀疏的白发在微微地颤动，满脸腾着白蒙蒙的汗水，我的心里涌起一阵酸楚。我上前把住了母亲的手："妈，不要擀了。"她回头看着我，笑着说："哪能呢，这是你从小最爱吃的。"说完，擦一把汗，又埋下头忙起来。听了母亲的话，我心里好惭愧，有很多地方我是对不起她老人家的……

　　母亲80岁那年，因为一场病，躺在炕上不能活动。我再回家时，就吃不到母亲的手擀面了。母亲好像欠了我们似的，"不行了，不能擀面条给你们吃了。"她眼里蓄满泪水叹着气说。我一边安慰她，一边暗暗地向母亲许诺：我一定会报答您的。

母亲过生日这天，我让弟妹们陪着母亲在炕上说话，自己便在厨房"大显身手"了。到吃饭时，我出其不意地向母亲献上了一碗长寿面。她吃了一口，惊奇地问："这面怎么和我擀的一样的味道，是谁的手艺?"我顽皮地翘起大拇指："当然是我了。"母亲怀疑地摇摇头，但当她看到我沾着面粉的双手时，眼里立刻放出了光彩："你什么时候学会了擀面条?"母亲哪里知道，为了让她在生日那天能吃到可口的寿面，我特意到一家面馆跟师傅学了两星期，回到家里又实践了好几次，终于在她生日的时候，给了她一个惊喜。母亲的脸，笑成了一朵花，连声地说着："好吃，好吃。"看着母亲舒心的样子，我感到幸福极了。

（文　程绍瑞）

【点评】

让我们像母亲牢记着我们的生日一样，牢记住母亲的生日，给母亲一个惊喜、一个回报。

Longevity Noodles for My Mother

Since I was a child, I have always loved the noodles my mother made. The long, thin noodles tasted smooth and chewy, especially with some sauce. Because of our family's situation, we had few chances to taste them. Fortunately, our neighbors always invited my mother to make noodles when they had some happy events like weddings or building new houses, and my mother would always bring back a bowl of noodles to satisfy my noodle craving.

Then I started to work away from home. Whenever I re-turned home, my mother would make noodles for me. A local custom held that "when a guest arrives, he will be treated with jiaozi (dumplings) and when he leaves, he will be treated with noodles." In this way, the long, thin noodles will grab the guests' heart. Seeing her working so hard with the big, long wooden rolling pin, with her thin gray hair trembling, I could not but beg, "Mom, please stop." My mother smiled back, "How can I? This is your favorite." Wiping her brow, she continued. When I heard what my mom said, I felt very ashamed for having let her down several times before.

When my mother was eighty years old, she fell ill and was unable to get up again. When she saw me return home, she said regrettably with tears in her eyes, "I am sorry. I am not able to make noodles for you anymore." Comforting my mother, I made a promise in my mind that I would return the good my mother had done for me.

On my mother's birthday, I asked my brother and sister to talk with our mother by her bed and went into the kitchen to make noodles for her. The Chinese have a tradition of making long, long noodles for birthdays to symbolize long life. I brought the noodles to my mother and she tasted them. Full of surprise, she asked, "They taste the same as the ones I make. Who made it?" I pointed at myself, "Of course it is me." Shaking her head, she didn't believe it at first. Then she saw the flour on my hands and she asked again in excitement, "When did you learn to make noodles?" I admitted that, in order to give my mother the best noodles on her birthday, I spent two weeks with a noodle cook and learned how to make good noodles. I also practiced several times at home before I gave my mother such a surprise. My mother smiled blissfully and said, "They are delicious. Very delicious."

Seeing my mother enjoying my noodles, I felt extremely happy.

(Cheng Shaorui)

【Comment】

Let us firmly memorize our mothers' birthdays just like they do our birthdays and give them a surprise in return.

慈母手中線
游子身上衣
臨行密密縫
意恐遲遲歸
誰言寸草心
報得三春暉

母子情

春夕畫畫唐人
孟郊詩立意

笑求年

邢振齡並題

二十五枚相思扣

　　我在上小学三年级时写的第一篇作文，被语文老师当着全班同学的面念了两遍。"写得不错。"他说，"加把劲，说不定你的文章也能印成铅字呢！"回家后我把这喜讯告诉了母亲。母亲的眉宇间溢满了欣慰的笑。

　　那时我家很穷，吃饭的人多，挣工分的人却少。母亲喂了几十只鸡，靠卖鸡蛋的钱，从集市上换来油盐酱醋，维持着一家人的生活。尽管生活清苦到了极点，母亲的脸上总还是挂着一抹浅笑，因为有一个从家门口路过的算命先生说，我命中注定了将来要靠笔杆子吃饭。这话于母亲，便是无数盏在前方闪耀的希望之灯。

　　从此我便开始投稿。稿纸和邮票是母亲从买油盐的钱里省出来的。我只是不计成败地一篇篇写，写了就誊。母亲义不容辞地承担了发信的任务，因为那时村里还没有邮筒，邮差也不愿步行几里山路到村里来。于是母亲出门的时候，总要问上一句："又写了作文没有？"

　　日子来去匆匆，整整一年，我连一封退稿信也没收到。希望，从大到小，又从小到无。我不知道，母亲每次是抱了多大的希望走向那个信件稀少的邮局，又是怎样一次次地看着女儿的梦从邮递员的手中跌落。我只知道，母亲每次回家看见倚在门前的我，眼中总饱含着许多许多的无奈和歉意，似乎我的作文发表不成，全是她做母亲的过错。

第一次发表文章时我已经上了初中。短短的几百字被印在市内的一家小报上。我没有订那份报纸，后来我才知道自己的名字变成了铅字。当时我在学校住读，母亲喜颠颠地赶到镇上，取回那5元钱的稿费。周末回家的时候，母亲捧给我一个精致的瓷罐。我摇摇瓷罐，只听见"稀里哗啦"的一片响。打开罐盖，发现里面装着一些1角的硬币，数了数，整整50枚！那是母亲跑了几个商店，赔尽了好话换来的。而这个精致的瓷罐，竟花了母亲6元钱！

捧着瓷罐，我觉得好沉好沉，鼻子酸酸的。我问母亲为什么这么爱给自己找麻烦，母亲只是笑，说道："妈心里高兴。"

以后的日子，无论到了什么地方，也无论有多少行李，我总是带着那个小瓷罐。

我考上大学的那一年，母亲正好50岁。那个冬天，大学校园里的女孩子找到了一种表达爱情的新方式。她们买来上好的丝线，取一枚硬币，用细丝线把硬币层层包裹起来，然后编成一枚美丽的相思扣，送给自己的恋人。

而我，只想把相思扣送给50岁的母亲。我取出床头的小瓷罐，第一次，把里面的硬币全倒了出来，还是整整50枚！我把它们做成了25枚相思扣，每个扣中包两枚硬币。

在那个夜深人静的晚上，当祝贺母亲生日的亲朋好友散去之后，我挨着母亲坐下。我叫母亲闭上眼睛，然后把那25枚五颜六色的相思扣都挂在了母亲的脖子上。母亲睁开眼，急急地要取下那些相思扣："鬼丫头，你这是干啥呀？把妈弄得老不

春屆拼百
蜂蝶舞
驅車踏青
扶阿母
舊地重游
柳成蔭
正是阿母
扶兒虛
甲申春夫
畫敬老故
事邢振齡
寫於圓緣堂

老少不少的像个什么样子?"

我按住母亲的手:"妈,您这大半辈子都活得像模像样,这一次,您就不像样一回吧!这些东西叫相思扣,是女孩子送给自己的心上人的。她们做的相思扣都是纯色的,而且中间只有一枚硬币,代表一心一意。可是妈妈,我给您做的相思扣用了两枚硬币,因为我觉得用双倍的情,也还不起我欠您的债……"

母亲搂着我,早已是热泪盈眶,不停地拍着我说:"够了,孩子,已经够了……"

(文 黄秀梅)

【点评】

双倍的孝心,也报答不尽母亲的养育之恩。

25 Love Buttons

I wrote my first composition in the third grade and it received widespread praise in my class. My teacher read it twice in front of the class and said, "It is well-written. Keep going and you will probably have your compositions put into print one day." I told this to my mother and she was brimming with smiles.

At that time, my family was very poor. My mother kept dozens of chickens and bought some daily necessaries from the market by selling eggs to support the family. Although we lived a very simple life, there was always a smile on her face. My mother was told once by a fortuneteller that I was destined to make a living by writing. This was to my mother like thousands of lights of hope ahead of her.

Since then, I began to write to newspapers and magazines. I bought paper and stamps with the money that my mother saved from buying cooking oil and salt. I kept writing and writing and my mother acted as the mail carrier. At that time, there was no mailbox in the village and the postman wouldn't walk the couple of miles in the mountains to our village either. Whenever my mother went out, she would ask me whether there were any manuscripts to be posted.

A whole year passed, I never received any letters about my manuscripts. My hope became smaller and smaller and even dim. I didn't know that every time my mother walked to the post office, she was full of hope, and then she would see her daughter's dreams gone from the postman's hands time and time again. What I knew was that every time my mother came back and saw me sitting against the door, she would feel very disappointed and sorry, as if it was all her fault that I didn't get my articles published.

I did not have any articles published until I entered the junior high school. One of my short articles was published in a small city newspaper. I didn't know it at first because I didn't subscribe to that newspaper. Later I learned that my name had finally made it into the newspaper. At that time I lived in the school. My mother hurried to town and fetched the author's remuneration, 5 yuan. When I returned home on the weekend, my mother gave me a delicate saving box. I shook it and heard some sounds. I opened it and found it was filled with 50 dimes, which my mother finally got by going to several stores to exchange the money. The saving box cost her 6 yuan!

Holding the saving box, I felt it very heavy and my eyes were dimmed with tears. I asked my mother why she took the trouble to do that, and she just smiled and said, "It made me happy."

From then on, I always kept the saving box with me, wherever I went and how heavy the luggage was.

The year I went to college, my mother turned 50. Girls in my school developed an idea of wrapping silk thread around coins one layer after another to express their love to their boyfriends.

For me, I just wanted to send love buttons to my 50-year-old mother. The first time, I poured out all 50 coins and made 25 love buttons, two coins in each button.

On the evening of my mother's birthday, after all the guests had left, I sat by my mother and asked her to shut her eyes. Then I put the string of 25 beautiful buttons around her neck. When my mother opened her eyes and saw the string, she felt uncomfortable. "You little naughty daughter, what is this for? I am too old to wear it!"

I put my hands on hers and said, "Mom, it is all right for you to feel uncomfortable just this time. These are called love buttons, which girls like to give to their boyfriends. They are just one color and there is only one coin in it, which means to give one's whole heart to his lover. But Mom, the buttons I gave you have two coins in each, because I don't think I could return your love even if I doubled the number."

My mother hugged me, tears in her eyes, and patted me, saying: "You have done enough, my dear."

(Huang Xiumei)

【Comment】

Even double your love and devotion is not enough to repay your mother's care and nurture for you.

中华敬老故事精选

Selected China Stories of Elder-Respecting

迟到的悔悟

　　我一直是一个乖顺听话的孩子，可是大学毕业的时候，却在分配问题上和爸爸发生了严重分歧，我要去西藏，爸爸坚决不同意。结果，我们父子之间"恩断义绝"。眼见一对父子紧张到互不相认的程度，原本沉默寡言的妈妈更加无话可说。

　　妈妈如果站在爸爸一边，也许我会好受些，可是她对我始终没有一句怨言。她的沉默既给了我莫大的勇气，又让我的心隐隐作痛。临行，妈妈默默地为我收拾行囊，看着她苍老而缓慢的背影，我差点改变主意。是啊，爸爸和妈妈日渐衰老，身边需要儿子的照顾。可是自古忠孝难以两全，为了自己的志向，我只能暂时做一个不孝之子了。

　　妈妈送我，好远好远，夏风吹干了妈妈的泪水，打湿了游子不安的心。终于到了巷口，我阻住了妈妈。妈妈站住，大颗大颗的泪涌了出来，她抬手帮我理了理头发说："你去那么远的地方，我不放心啊，多写信回来，妈妈等你……"

　　终于到了我梦中的西藏。几年之间，我的足迹几乎踏遍了雪域高原。我只陶醉在这青天碧水和崇山峻岭之中，几乎忽略了远方妈妈的存在。不知不觉间，我对妈妈的孝心已经变成了薄薄的信纸和每逢节假日时寄回去的钞票。妈妈的信总是写满了思念和牵挂，她告诉我不要寄钱，她不需要钱，惟愿我早日平安归来。

被雪山远远阻隔的时空在我对亲情和孝心的荒疏中很快划过了5个年头。我和爸爸的关系始终没有像妈妈所期待的那样完全解冻，这成了她最大的心病。

去年春天，妈妈的信突然断了。那段时间我去了可可西里，回到拉萨发现妈妈已近两个月没有来信。我慌了，赶紧打电话，电话那端传来爸爸急切的声音："再不赶快回来就看不到你妈妈了……"天啊，妈妈病危！我以最快的速度踏上归途，心里只有一个念头：妈妈，您一定要等我回来……

可是，妈妈终是没能等到我。当晚8点多一点的时候，在飞机上，我突然感到一阵剧烈的头痛，眼前一片漆黑。恍惚中，我看到妈妈瘦弱的身影向我飘来，冲我凄然一笑就不见了。到家以后，爸爸告诉我，妈妈果然在那时去世。她已经撑了好几天，死前口中仍念着我的乳名。

爸爸流着泪带我来到院子当中，递给我一把铁锹，指着那棵老杏树说："挖开吧。"在杏树旁，我满腹疑云地挖开一个插有标记的地方，很快，一个褐色的陶罐子出现在我的眼前。捧出罐，打开盖子，我惊呆了！里面是一叠用塑料布包得严严实实的钞票，还有捆扎得整整齐齐的几年来我寄给妈妈的信。爸爸哽咽着说："你寄来的钱，你妈妈一分不少地存放在这里。"捧着这些钱和信，我失声痛哭："妈妈啊，难道这就是我几年来的孝心？五年啦，就是工作再忙，也应当回来看看您哪！我犯了一个天大的错误啊！"我将这些信在妈妈灵前点燃：妈妈，请您在遥远的天国接受儿子迟到的忏悔吧！

（文 冠 嘉）

【点评】

儿女是风筝，父母是线。当牵着我们的丝线突然扯断，放飞的我们才会感到心无所依，痛悔终生。好好孝敬你的双亲吧，不要放过每一个机会。

Belated Repentance

I had always been an obedient child until I graduated from college. I insisted on going to Tibet, but my father disagreed. As a result, we almost broke up our relationship. Between us, my mother had to keep silent.

If my mother stood on my father's side, I would have felt better, but she didn't blame me at all. My mother's silence gave me courage and a dull pain at the same time. Prior to my setting off, my mother silently packed my things. Looking at my slow, elderly mom, I almost changed my mind. It was true that my parents were getting older and needed their son around to take care of them. But for the sake of my ambition, I had to put my filial piety aside and disobey my father to go my own way.

My mother went a long way to see me off, both of us feeling sad. Finally I stopped her. Before parting, she tidied my hair and said with tears in her eyes: "Tibet is very far away. I will worry about you. Remember to write often. Mom waits for you..."

At last, my dream came true. For several years, I left my footprints all over the snow-covered highland. I was so immersed in this beautiful place that I had almost forgotten the existence of my mother. Without noticing, my love and devotion to my mother became a thin piece of paper and some money I sent home during the holidays. My mother's letters were always full of worries and missing. She asked me not to send money home any more, because they had enough. She only hoped that I would return safe and sound.

Soon, five years passed, and my relations with my father did not ease as my mother had expected and this became her biggest worry.

Last spring, my mother suddenly stopped writing me letters. At that time, I was in Kekexili Desert and when I returned to Lhasa, it had already been two months since I received the last letter from her. I became worried and immediately called home. At the other end, there was my father's voice, "If you do not hurry back, you probably will not be able to see your mother again." I was startled. I immediately flew back home, hoping that my mother would wait for me.

However, my mother didn't see me in her last moment. Just past eight in the evening that night, I felt a sudden headache on the plane and I saw nothing but darkness in front of me. It seemed that I saw my thin mother floating toward me and smiling at me before disappearing. When I arrived home, my father told me that she had passed away at a little past eight, just the time when I felt the sudden headache. She had stayed on for several days, murmuring my infant name.

My father, tears in eyes, took me to the courtyard, handed

学步图

母子情

漫漫人生路
始于初学步
儿女长成材
父母心血护

甲申春无画故老之事 邢振龄作

me a shovel, and asked me to dig under the apricot tree. Soon, a brown clay jar appeared. I opened it and was startled to see in it the money and letters I had sent to her, carefully wrapped in a plastic bag. My father sobbed, "Your mother kept every cent you sent." Holding the money and letters, I cried my heart out, "Where is my filial piety? It has been five years. I should have been able to come back to see you, no matter how busy I was. Now I have made an unforgivable mistake!" I burned the letters in front of the memorial tablet of my mother, crying, "Mom, in heaven far away, please accept this belated repentance from your son! "

(Guan Jia)

【Comment】

Children are like kites and parents strings. When the strings are suddenly broken, children will feel they have nowhere to turn and feel regret for the rest of their lives. Show your love and devotion to your parents and do not let any chance slip by.

七十岁的父亲和
九十岁的爷爷

　　我的父亲70多岁了，我的爷爷已经90多岁高龄了。父亲的许多朋友和同事都很羡慕地对父亲说："你可真有福气，70多岁了还有一个老爹，还能叫上一声'爸爸'!"父亲笑呵呵地回答："是啊，是啊，这是人生中一大快事喽!"

　　90多岁的爷爷身体非常健康，有时我们一家人都感冒，他老人家却连一个喷嚏都不打。爷爷的耳朵特别大，慈眉善目，头发和胡须雪白，挺着硬朗的腰板坐在那儿，活脱脱一个老寿星。

　　70多岁的父亲在90多岁的爷爷眼里依然是个孩子。吃饭时，大家把最好的菜放在爷爷面前，他却总是推到父亲那儿，用筷子夹着菜，不停地放到父亲的碗里，不住声地唠叨："吃吧，快吃吧。"父亲把菜推回去，他又很不高兴地推过来。每每这时，父亲只好依着爷爷，大口大口吃着，很夸张地吧唧着嘴，很香甜地咀嚼着。看到父亲这种吃相，坐在旁边的爷爷会露出满意的笑容。

90多岁的爷爷对70多岁的父亲有着孩子般的依赖。爷爷每天早晨醒来的时候，就会喊父亲的名字，如果父亲不在，他就会坐立不安，在你耳边嘀咕："长兴上哪儿去啦？他怎么还不回来呀？"爷爷的耳朵不太灵光了，每与他说话，都要拼尽丹田之气，像打雷一样，震天动地。我们轮番上阵向爷爷解释父亲的去向，爷爷总是一脸的焦急，再加点茫然，还是问我们："怎么着？长兴上哪儿去了？"如果再见不到父亲，爷爷就会发火，撺着家里人到外面去找。那时他胡子也哆嗦，手也颤抖，跟在你屁股后面追问："你爹呢？你也不知道他上哪儿去了？还不快去找找！"父亲有事不回来，爷爷就不吃饭，坐在那儿等着他。一直到父亲回家，爷爷虎着的脸上才会有喜色。并叨叨着埋怨父亲："你上哪儿去了？怎么才回来？我等着你吃饭哩！"

　　人在孩童时代，最依恋的就是自己的父母，父母温暖的胸膛就是他们最好的避风港。同样，父母老了，也会返回童年时代，需要依偎在儿女的胸口，需要儿女们年轻挺拔的身姿，能为像秋天枯草一样衰老的他们，支撑起晴空朗朗、鲜花满园的天地。

（文　高阳）

【点评】

　　在父母眼里，儿女再大也是孩子；在儿女眼里，父母越老越是财富。怎样关爱自己的儿女，就该怎样关爱自己的父母。

搔痒圖

小竹搔搔
只把長
怎及小手
搔痒：搔
我是爺：
痒：搔
搔在爺：
心坎上
祖孫情

甲申春天寫
邢振齡作

70–Year–Old Dad and 90–Year–Old Grandpa

My father is over 70 and my grandpa is over 90.   Many of my father's friends admire him a lot.   They say, "You are really lucky to still have your father and you can have someone to call 'Father' ! "   "You are right," my father would say with a smile. "This is one of the happiest things in my life."

My 90–year–old grandpa is in robust health.   When every one of us catches a cold, nothing happens to him at all.   My grandpa has very big ears, a kind face, gray hair, and a grizzled beard. He sits very straight and looks just like the god of longevity.

In the eyes of my grandpa, my father is still a child.   At the dinner table,   when everyone puts the best food in front of him, he will push it toward my father, adding,   "Eat this, my son." He will push the dish back   sulkily if my father tries to move it to Grandpa.   Then my father will have to gobble the food.   When-ever my grandpa sees this, his face brims over with smiles.

My grandpa seems quite dependent on my father.   Every day

when he gets up, he will call my father's name. If he is not around, he will ask us anxiously "Where is Changxing? Why isn't he back by now? " My grandpa is a little deaf, so every time we talk to him, we need to use all our strength to shout like thunder. We explain in turns to grandpa where my father has gone, but he still remains worried and confused, and asks us, "What? Where has my son gone?" If my father still doesn't show up, he will get very angry, urging everyone to look for him. His beard and hands will tremble and he will keep asking, "Where is your father? You don't know where he has gone either? Why don't you go right away to find him?" My grandpa will refuse to eat without seeing my father and keep waiting until my father comes back. Then he will be happy again and com-plain to my father, "Where have you been? How come you came back so late? I was waiting for you."

One always relies on his parents in childhood. A parent's embrace is the best haven. When parents get old, they seem to return to their childhood and they are eager to fall into the em-brace of their children as well. They need their young children to bring them the happiness and the brightness of life.

(Gao Yang)

【Comment】

In the eyes of parents, children are always children no mat-ter how old they are. But in the eyes of children, parents are a wealth of wisdom and experience. We should love our parents the same way we love our children.

珍贵的戒指

父亲已有四五天未进汤水了。看来，最后的时刻快到了。

儿女媳婿孙辈全齐了，几乎满满一屋人。千呼万唤，父亲依然安睡。

输液管在嘀嗒、嘀嗒地落泪。

妈妈去得早，丢下一群儿女。家境贫寒，记忆中的父亲整日都为生计奔命。

中年丧偶，晚境寂寞。我们一天天长大，一个接一个拍拍屁股走了。于是劝父亲娶个老伴……父亲无语。

第二天，他从箱底翻出妈妈的大照片，放进床头的镜框里。

我是幺女，被父亲视为掌上珠。哥姐们成家走后，我们相依为命。父亲常说我是个懂事的孩子。

记得我要出嫁那几天，父亲因买不起一枚戒指送我而暗自伤神。我赶紧安慰老人，说你已经尽了全力，你把我们拉扯大多不容易。想到将远走他乡，不能再守在爸爸身旁尽孝，报答他老人家的养育之恩，我放声哭了，父亲又反过来强作欢颜哄我……

父亲从昏迷中苏醒过来，半睁双眼，环顾他的儿孙们，老眼里放出一种奇异的光芒。他的嘴动了几下，但已说不出一句话，他便伸出瘦骨嶙峋的手，一个一个地抚摸……

轮到我了，我感到父亲的手颤动得格外厉害，我捧住那只摇动的干枯的手，虔诚地缓慢跪下了。

我们用手交流着千言万语。

父亲轻轻摩挲着我的手背，然后又轻轻抚摸着我的手掌，在长茧花的地方摸了许多遍，最后他的手停在我右手的无名指上，停了许久许久……我抬起泪眼望着他，蒙眬中父亲眼眶中也泪光闪闪，他的嘴抽搐不停，一定在说什么，脸上的皱纹挤在一处。

我当然清楚父亲此刻的心事，忙把他冰凉的手紧紧贴在我滚烫的面颊上。

父亲抽回手，只见他在干瘪的嘴里掏了半天，竟掏出一颗金牙，蓦地按在我的手心……这一幕把所有的人都惊呆了。

我们都望着那颗金牙。

这大概是我们的父亲、也是我们这个家惟一的一块黄金了。

父亲去了，没有留下遗嘱；而我们除了泪，也无别的表示。

若干年后，我用父亲的金牙打了一枚戒指，戴着去为他老人家扫墓。

大哥问我："小妹，你知道父亲这颗金牙的来历吗？"我摇头。

大哥告诉我："那是母亲卖了自己的戒指为他安的……那年我16岁，你才6岁。"

我把那金晃晃的圆环放在掌心，它忽然变成了爸爸的金牙，当我拈起它时，它一下子又变成了妈妈的戒指……忍不住，我"哇"地一声大哭起来。

（文　张凤兰）

【点评】

　　黄金有价，亲情无价。一枚小小的戒指，演绎着一家人相濡以沫的真情。

An Invaluable Ring

My father had not eaten anything for four or five days. It seemed that the end of his life was approaching.

The whole family came and crowded into this small room. Despite their calling to him, my father was still sleeping calmly.

The transfusion tube was dripping like tears.

My mother died early, leaving all the children to my father. Our family was poor, so my father rushed around for a living all the time.

The death of my mother brought my father loneliness. As we children had grown up one after another and gone away from home, we started to suggest that my father find a companion. But he just kept silent.

The second day, he dug out a big picture of my mother from the chest and put it into the frame by his bed.

I'm the youngest in the family, like a pearl in my father's hand. When my brothers and sisters all married, I was left at home to live with my father and we supported each other. He often told me that I was a good girl.

I remember the day when I got married. My father felt very sad, as he could not buy a ring for me. I comforted him, saying that he had already done his best by bringing up all his children. When I thought that I would leave my father and couldn't stay with him to return his love and care, I cried, then my father put on an air of cheerfulness and tried to comfort me.

My father woke up from the coma, looking around with eyes half open, emitting a strange glow. His mouth moved a little, but no words came out. He just stretched out one of his skinny hands to touch his children.

When my turn came, I felt his hand trembling. I cupped his hand and knelt down before his bed. In this way my father and I communicated heart to heart.

My father lightly ran his hand over the backs of my hands, felt back and forth the callus on my palms, and stopped at my ring finger for quite a while. Tears seemed to roll down his cheeks. His mouth was twitching and I knew he was trying to say something.

I knew how my father felt and moved his cold hands to my warm cheeks.

He withdrew his hand, felt for something in his mouth for a while, and finally took out one gold tooth and put it into my hand. Everyone was startled.

We all looked at the gold tooth. This might be the only piece of gold in our family.

My father passed away, leaving nothing. We could express nothing but tears.

Several years passed.   I had a ring made out of the gold tooth and wore it to visit my father's grave.

My elder brother asked me, "Sister, do you know anything about the gold tooth? "   I shook my head.

He continued, "Our mother sold her ring for the gold tooth of our father when I was 16 years old and you were 6."

I put the ring on my palm.   Suddenly it turned into Father's gold tooth,   and then Mother's ring when I touched it.   I could not but let out a cry...

(Zhang Fenglan)

【Comment】

Gold has its value, but family affection is priceless. A small ring tells the true feelings of an entire family.

牵着母亲过马路

真是"树大分丫，儿大分家"。有了自己的营垒，精力便全部倾注于家庭。虽说和父母同城而居，相隔不远，却很少回家看望他们。

周末下午，我携妻儿回家，年近花甲的母亲喜不自禁，一定要上街买点好菜招待我们。妻一再相劝，母亲却执意要去。母亲说："你们别拦了，你们回来，妈给你们煮饭，不是受累，是高兴呀！"我说："我陪您去吧！"母亲乐呵呵地说："好，好，你去，你说买啥，妈就买啥。"

到菜市需要走一段人行道，再横穿一条马路。正是下班时间，大街上车来车往，川流不息的人群匆匆而行。毕竟年纪大了，母亲的双腿显得不那么利索，走路怎么也快不起来。她提着菜篮，挨着我边走边谈些家长里短的生活琐事。我宽容地耐心听着。树老根多，人老话多。母亲这把年纪，自然爱絮絮叨叨，别人不愿听，儿女们还能不听？哪怕装也要装出忠实听众的样子才行。

夕阳缓缓傍近西山，如同节日的红灯笼。桔红色的光芒，染红了母亲慈祥的脸庞，映衬出她老人家脸上那饱经沧桑的岁月。

穿过马路，就是菜市了。母亲突然停下来，她把菜篮挎在臂弯，腾出右手，向我伸来……

刹那间，我的心灵震颤起来……

上小学时，我每天都要横穿一条马路才能到学校。那时在城东印刷厂工作的母亲，怕我过马路出事，每天都要把我送过马路后才急匆匆赶去上班。而每次她总是把我的小手握在她的掌心，生怕有个闪失。直到分手，她还一遍遍叮嘱："有车来就别过马路，过马路要跟着别人一起过。"匆匆的人流，喧嚣的市声，那一幅母爱图显得何其平淡，却又何其伟大。

20多年过去了，昔日的小手已长成一双男子汉的大手；昔日的泥石公路已变成柏油马路，昔日的母亲也已是皱纹满面、步履蹒跚，只是那双牵着儿女手的动作仍是那么温馨娴熟。她一生为了儿女吃了许多苦，受了许多罪，这些都被她掠头发一样——掠散，但是掠不掉的是爱子的真情。可是，她一生细细呵护的儿子，却对她日渐淡漠。

我没有把手递过去，而是从她臂弯上取下篮子，并轻轻握住她的手说："妈，小时候，都是您牵着我过马路，今天让我也牵您一回，好吗?"母亲一怔，脸上笑容随即荡漾开来。

"妈，您腿脚不灵便，车多人又挤，过马路时千万要前后左右看一看，别跟车抢时间。啥时家里有事，只要需要，不管多远多忙，我们都会来。跟您一把屎一把尿拉扯大的儿子，您还客气啥?"母亲背过头去，默默地揩着泪水。

牵着母亲过马路，心里几许感激，几许心疼，几许爱意，还有几许感叹。

（文 明 锋）

【点评】

据说，"孝"这个字在甲骨文里的写法，是一个少年牵着一位老人的手，慢慢地走。生命的两头，人人需要牵手。

Guiding My Mother
Across the Street

There exists an old saying that trees will branch out when getting bigger, and children will set up their own families when grown up. Finally I had my own family and started to pay more attention to my family. Although my parents and I live in the same city and not far away, I seldom visit them.

One weekend afternoon, I took my family home to see my mother. My mother felt very happy and insisted on going to the market to buy some good food to treat us. My wife tried to stop her, but my mother was determined. She said, "Don't feel bad. I am happy to be able to cook for you." Then I said, "Let me go with you." My mother answered with a smile, "Good, good. You come with me. Mom will buy whatever you want to eat."

To get to the market, we needed to walk along the sidewalk for a while and then cross a road. It was right at rush hour and the streets were crowded with vehicles and people. My mother was old, so she couldn't walk very fast. Carrying her basket, she started to tell me all trivial household affairs. I listened to her patiently. Old people always have more to talk about, just like old trees have more roots. It was the same with my mom. However, I, as her child, would still listen to her even if others didn't want to. At least I tried to be a good listener to make her happy.

It was dusk. The sun was setting in the west like a red lantern. The sunshine on my mother's face reflected her life full of hardships.

We came to the road, across which lay the market. My mother suddenly stopped. She hooked the basket over her left arm and stretched out her right arm to me.

At once my heart started to quiver.

When I was in primary school, I needed to cross a road every day to go to school. My mother worked in a printing factory east of the city. Every day, to keep me safe, she would take my little hand in hers and hold it tightly to cross the road before going to work. Every time she would warn me, "Don't cross the road if you see a car coming. You can follow others when you cross the road." A mother's love is so ordinary, yet so great.

Now more than two decades have passed. The once small hands have become the big hands of a man. The mud and gravel road has been paved. My mother's face is full of wrinkles and her legs are not as flexible as before, but she is just as skilled at taking a child's hand. She has been working hard all her life for her children. No one knows how much suffering she has sustained. But she has brushed aside all these just like she brushed her hair.   The only thing she didn't sweep away was her love for her son.   But it seemed my love for my mother had been thinning out.

I didn't reach out my hand.   Instead,   I took the vegetable basket from her arm and gently clasped her hand.   "Mom, when I was young,   you always took me across the road.   Now I will guide you across the road."   I said to her.   My mother was surprised and then smiled.

"Mom,   since it is hard for you to move around and there are so many vehicles and people,   you must look around before you cross the road.   Take it easy.   Whenever there is a need, we will come to help.   Your son is here, ready to help you anytime. Just let me know."   My mother tilted her head back and silently wiped her tears.

Holding my mother's hand to cross the road,   I felt much gratitude,   much sorrow,   much care,   and much tenderness in my heart.

(Ming Feng)

【Comment】

It is said that the Chinese character for "piety" is written pictographically as a child leading an old man in the ancient times.   At both the beginning and end of life, everyone needs a hand.

爱 的 针 法

一次，在一位朋友家小坐。发现他给父母打电话的时候拨了两遍号码。第一遍拨过之后，铃响三声就挂断，再拨第二遍，然后通话。

"第一遍占线吗?"我随意问。

"没有。"

"是没想好说什么?"

"不是。"

"那干吗拨两遍号?"

他笑了笑："你不知道，我爸爸妈妈都是接电话非常急的人，只要听见铃响，就会跑着去接。有一次，妈妈为接电话还让桌腿把小脚趾绊了一下，肿了很长时间。从那时起，我就和二老约定，接电话不准跑。我先拨一遍，给他们预备的时间。"

我心里忽然有一种温暖而湿润的感觉。平日都常说如何如何孝敬父母，这个小小的细节，不是对父母最生动的疼爱吗?"爱"是一件大衣衫，衣衫是要讲究式样、色彩、衣料，甚至于时尚和流行的程度的。但是,对于穿衣服的人来说,更需要这样细密而熨帖的针法,才能让这件衣衫变得真正温暖舒适起来啊。

为了让父母多一份安全和从容，多拨一遍电话号码，这是一件再琐碎不过的小事。可是，这一小事就是爱的针法！

（文 乔 叶）

【点评】

细微之处见孝心。儿女的一个细心，便会让父母收益无穷。

Needlework of Love

Once, I went to visit my friend. I found that when he called his parents, he dialed twice. The first time he hung up the phone after the phone rang three times. The second time he dialed and spoke.

"Was the line busy the first time you dialed? " I asked, curious.

"No." he said.

"Then, you did not know what to say at first? "

"No." my friend said.

"Then why did you dial twice? " I pursued.

He smiled, saying, "You know, whenever my parents heard the ringing of the phone, they would come to pick it up in a rush." Once my mother bumped into a small chair and hurt her little toe. It took quite a long time to get well. From then on, we agreed that there was no more need to rush for the phone. I would dial once as a signal so that they would have enough time to get prepared.

Suddenly a warm and comforting feeling came into my mind.

We always talk about how to show our filial piety to our parents, but I have never seen such an example; it is a symbol of our deepest love for our parents. Love is like a shirt: it needs the appropriate style, color, and material; it even needs to be trendy. But to the one who wears the shirt, the delicate needlework is the most important part, in order to make them feel truly warm and comfortable.

It is a minute detail in life to dial twice for the sake of the safety and ease of parents. It is like the needlework of love.

(Qiao Ye)

【Comment】

Piety can be expressed in the tiniest details. Meticulousness of children will be of great help to their parents.

第一次抱母亲

母亲病了，住在医院里，我们兄弟姐妹轮流去守护母亲。轮到我守护母亲那天，护士进来换床单，叫母亲起来，母亲病得不轻，下床很吃力。我赶紧说："妈，您别动，我来抱您。"

我左手揽住母亲的脖子，右手揽住她的腿弯，使劲一抱，没想到母亲轻轻的，我用力过猛，差点朝后摔倒。

护士在后面托了我一把，责怪说："你使那么大劲干什么？"我说："我没想到我妈这么轻。"护士问："你以为你妈有多重？"我说："我以为我妈有 100 多斤。"护士笑了，说："你妈这么矮小，别说病成这样，就是年轻力壮的时候，我猜她也到不了 90 斤。"母亲说："这位姑娘有眼力，我这一生，最重的时候只有 89 斤。"

母亲竟然这么轻，我心里很难过。护士取笑我说："亏你和你妈生活了几十年，眼力这么差。"我说："如果你和我妈生活几十年，你也会看不准的。"护士问："为什么？"我说："在我的记忆中，母亲总是手里拉着我，背上背着妹妹，肩上再挑着 100 多斤的担子翻山越岭。这样年复一年，直到我们长大后，可以干活了。但每逢有重担，母亲总是叫我们放下，让她来挑。我一直以为母亲力大无穷，没想到她是用 80 多斤的身体，去承受那么多重担。"

我望着母亲瘦小的脸，愧疚地说："妈，我对不住您啊！"

护士也动情地说："大妈，你真了不起。"

母亲笑一笑说："提那些事干什么，哪个母亲不是这样过来的?"护士把旧床单拿走，铺上新床单，又很小心地把边边角角拉平，然后回头吩咐我："把大妈放上去吧，轻一点。"

我突发奇想地说："妈，你把我从小抱到大，我还没有好好抱你一回呢。让我抱你入睡吧。"母亲说："快把我放下，别让人笑话。"护士说："大妈，你就让他抱一回吧。"母亲这才没有做声。

我坐在床沿上，把母亲抱在怀里，就像小时候母亲无数次抱我那样。

母亲终于闭上眼睛。我以为母亲睡着了，准备把她放到床上去，可是，我看见有两行泪水，从母亲的眼里流了出来……

（文　张炜月）

【点评】

妈妈把儿女从小抱大，谁又曾抱过妈妈？当儿女抱起弥留中的妈妈，她的泪水为什么会潸潸流下？

Carrying Mother
for the First Time

My mother became ill and was hospitalized. My siblings and I took turns nursing her. On the day when it was my turn, a nurse came in to change the sheets. She asked my mother to get up, but my mother was so sick that it was very difficult for her to get out of bed. I hastened to comfort her, "Mom, please don't move. I will carry you."

· I supported her neck with my left hand and held her legs with the right, and prepared myself for a heavy lift. I had never expected her to be so light, I overexerted that I almost fell backward when I lifted her.

According to the nurse, my mother had weighed only 45 kilograms.

I felt very sad about this, because during her illness, her weight dropped even lower. I remembered that when we climbed the mountain, my mother always took my hand and carried my sister on her back, and she placed more than 50 kilograms of weight on her shoulders. Year in and year out, as we grew up, she still insisted that she shoulder the heavy burdens. In my mind, she had inexhaustible strength. However, I had never ex-pected that she would weigh so little.

Looking at the scraggy face of my mother, I felt ashamed of myself. "Mom, I feel guilty." I mumbled.

The nurse became excited, "Aunt, you are so great."

My mother smiled and said, "That is the duty of every moth-er." The nurse finished making the bed. "You may place your mother back in bed now. Be careful."

Suddenly a strange idea occurred to me. "Mom, let me hold you and put you to sleep, just like you did for me when I was a child."

I sat on the edge of the bed and held my mother.

She closed her eyes. I thought she had gone to sleep. When I laid her on the pillow, I saw tears rolling down her cheeks.

(Zhang Weiyue)

【Comment】

A mother holds her children until they grow up. However, who holds his mother just as she held her child? When a child holds his mother as she is dying, why does she weep?

跳个舞唱只歌

我陪奶奶找乐：

我和奶奶：

奶奶玩翻撑

奶奶乐得咯……

甲申年春天

画故老故事　祖孙情　邢振龄作

虞舜孝顺父母

虞舜，字重华，是中国父系社会后期部落联盟的首领。

舜小的时候，他的母亲就死了，父亲又娶了个后妻，生了个弟弟叫象。舜是个好孩子，勤劳诚恳，孝敬父母，家里的活都是他干。可是继母心地狭窄、泼辣蛮横，弟弟象也很自私自利。

有一天，象和母亲商量想害死舜。他们叫舜修整漏雨的仓屋。舜虽隐隐约约觉察出他们的用意，但还是答应了。他带着两只斗笠，顺着梯子爬上仓顶，认真地修补起来。

这时，象偷偷地走近仓屋，悄悄地把梯子扛走，然后又放了一把火。顿时，茅草盖的仓屋燃烧起来，火舌席卷，浓烟滚滚，舜急忙寻找梯子，但梯子已找不到了。于是他把两只斗笠挟在腋下，像插上鸟的翅膀，乘着风势，跳了下来。

象和继母见一计不成，又生一计。他们叫舜去修井。舜还是答应了，这次他带了两把短斧。舜下井后，并没有先掏泥沙，而是在井壁上挖了一个洞，这个洞紧挨着邻居家另一口井的通道。舜刚挖好，象就在井上叫他了。舜的答声未落，泥团石块就像下雨一样落了下来，一会儿就把井填满了。舜由于躲进刚挖好的洞里，才没有遇害。过了一会儿，舜从邻居家的井口爬了出来。他没有回家，只身来到历山脚下，开荒种地过日子。

有一年，发生了自然灾害。舜的父母因遭灾，生活发生了困难。父亲十分想念儿子舜，常常独自一人到那口被填满的井边哭泣，慢慢地眼睛哭瞎了。继母也变得神情迟钝，象则成了哑巴。

有一天，舜的继母挑了一担柴到集市上换米，正巧舜也去卖米，他认出了继母。舜把米给她，故意没有收柴，一连几天都是这样。继母把这件事告诉了舜的父亲。父亲想，天下哪有这样的好人，只有儿子舜才会这样做。可是继母不信，说："百尺井底又有大石头压着，哪能活下来呢？"

父亲坚持要去看一看。第二天，继母和象扶着舜的父亲来到集市，他们故意站在舜的身边。父亲听了一会儿，对舜说："听你的声音像是我儿子。"舜回答说："我就是舜啊！"他上前抱住父亲哭了，父亲也放声大哭起来。后来，舜把父母和兄弟都接回了家。传说，尧帝听了这件事，非常赞赏舜的品德，他把自己的两个女儿嫁给了舜，还将帝位禅让给他。

【点评】

面对继母的歹心，无怨无恨，并在继母年迈之时，悉心赡养，义无反顾。敬老文化，始于虞舜，源远流长。

Yu Shun – an
Example of Filial Piety

Yu Shun, also known as Zhong Hua, was a chieftain of a clan alliance during the latter part of the Chinese patriarchal period.

His mother died when Shun was a child. His father married again and Shun's stepmother gave birth to a child named Xiang. Shun was a good boy, industrious and filial to his parents. He did all the house chores. But his stepmother was narrow-minded and tyrannical, and his brother, Xiang, was also very selfish.

One day, Xiang and his mother plotted to kill Shun. They asked Shun to repair a warehouse roof. Sensing their intention, Shun took two straw hats with him and climbed up to the roof, starting to repair it.

Just then, Xiang sneaked close to the house, took the ladder away and set the warehouse on fire. At once the house started burning heavily, dark smoke billowing. Shun rushed to look for the ladder but it was gone. Then he placed the two straw hats under his arms, like two wings, and jumped off the roof.

After the failure, Xiang and his mother thought of another plot. They asked Shun to repair the well. Shun obeyed. This time, he took two axes with him. He didn't dig out the mud and sand in the well right away. Instead, he first dug a hole on the wall of the well that led to the well of his neighbor. When he had just finished, Xiang called him. No sooner had Shun answered than a rain of stones and mud fell into the well. In no time, the well was filled up. This time Shun survived by hiding in the hole of the wall.

After a while, Shun climbed up out of the neighbor's well. He did not return home, but went up the hill and began to farm a piece of uncultivated land for a living.

One year a natural disaster struck. Shun's parents lived a hard life because of the disaster. His father missed Shun very much. He was often seen crying by the filled-up well. Soon he became blind and his stepmother became mentally slow. Xiang turned into a mute.

One day, Shun's stepmother took some firewood to the rural bazaar to exchange for some rice. It happened that Shun was selling rice there. He recognized his stepmother but kept silent. He gave some rice to her, without taking her firewood. This repeated several times. His stepmother told this to his father. His father said that only his son could do this. But the stepmother did not believe it, and she said, "It was impossible for Shun to survive at the bottom of the well. The deep well is full of rocks."

But his father insisted on going to the bazaar to have a look. The next day, Shun's stepmother and Xiang took his father to the bazaar. They stood by Shun. After a while, his father said to Shun, "Your voice sounded like my son's." Shun answered, "I'm your son, Shun!" He clasped his father and cried and so did his father. Later on, Shun took both his parents and his brother to his home. According to the legend, when Emperor Yao heard this, he spoke highly of Shun's morality. Later he married two of his daughters to Shun and made Shun his successor.

【Comment】

Despite the evil intentions of his stepmother, Shun did not have any hatred for her. When she became advanced in age, he meticulously took care of her. This culture of respecting elders began with Shun and has lasted the test of time.

原 谷 背 篓

　　原谷是春秋时陈留一带人。他9岁时，祖父已经年老不能耕作了，父母厌恶祖父，商议将祖父丢弃荒郊野外。原谷听说后，跪在双亲面前求情，遭到斥责。

　　次日凌晨，父亲命原谷抬篓，把祖父丢弃荒野。在路上，原谷抬着篓子走在前面，一边走一边回头望望祖父。风烛残年的祖父坐在篓子里，神情暗淡，表情呆滞，注视着频频回头的孙子。

　　将老人抬到荒野后，父亲命原谷抛掉篓子回家。原谷不仅不抛掉篓子，反而把篓子紧紧地背在了身上。父亲不解地问："要这个破篓子干啥？"原谷一本正经地回答："等你年老了不能耕作时，我好用它把你也送到这里来。"

　　父亲听了当即怒斥他："小孩子，怎么能跟大人说这种话？"

　　原谷反驳道："儿子应当听从父亲的教诲。你能这样对待爷爷，我为什么就不能用同样的方法对待你呢？"

　　原谷的话使父亲大为震惊，继而羞愧难当。他跪倒在父亲面前哭求饶恕，带着愧色将老人抬回家中，精心赡养，孝敬终身。

【点评】

"己所不欲，勿施于人。"聪明的原谷用"换位教育法"，让不孝的父母幡然醒悟。

Yuan Gu Saves His Grandpa

It was the Spring and Autumn period (a Chinese dynasty between 770–476 BC). When Yuan Gu, a native of Chenliu, was nine years old, his grandpa was already too old to work in the fields. His parents got tired of the old man and discussed abandoning him in the wilderness. When Yuan Gu heard about it, he knelt down in front of his parents, begging them not to do so. But he was rebuked.

Early in the morning the next day, Yuan Gu was ordered by his father to put his grandpa in a basket and abandon him in the wild. On the way, Yuan Gu frequently turned back to his grandpa and his very old grandpa in the basket gazed back at Yuan Gu with vacant look and lifeless facial expression.

When they reached a barren field, his father ordered him to leave the basket there and go home. But Yuan Gu refused. He clasped the basket. His father was confused, "What do you want with that shabby basket? " Yuan Gu answered seriously, "When you are old and unable to do field work, I could use the same basket to bring you here."

Hearing that, his father scolded him right away, "You little boy, how dare you speak like this to your father? "

But Yuan Gu argued, "As your son, I should listen to you. Since you can treat your father like this, why can't I do the same to you? "

His father was shocked to hear that and felt very ashamed of himself. He knelt down before his helpless old father, begging for forgiveness. He took the old man home and meticulously took care of him until his death.

【Comment】

Do not do unto others what you would not have them do unto you. The smart Yuan Gu succeeded in convincing his father by placing him in the position of his grandpa.

子骞劝父谅后母

　　闵子骞是春秋时期鲁国人，孔子的学生。

　　子骞从小就死了生母，父亲娶了后妻，成为他的继母。子骞年纪虽小，却孝顺父母。平时吃饭，他总是恭敬地把好饭菜端到父母面前，吃完饭后，他又抢着收拾桌子，洗刷碗筷。后来，继母接连生了两个弟弟，子骞的日子从此便不好过了。他像奴仆一样被使来唤去，白天要带弟弟玩耍，晚上要哄弟弟睡觉。继母稍不顺心，就又打又骂。

　　一个严寒的冬日，子骞给父亲赶车。大风夹着碎雪打来，把他冻得瑟瑟发抖，手上的缰绳老掉到地上。父亲呵斥他做事不专心，子骞一句话也不分辩。可冻僵的双手还是拉不住缰绳。父亲看看儿子身上穿的棉衣，觉得厚厚的，怎么会冷成这样？一定是儿子装的，没出息！父亲生气地一鞭子打了下去。棉衣当即裂开了一个大口子，一团团芦花露了出来，被风吹走。父亲大吃一惊，怎么后妻竟干出这种事？他带着子骞驾车返回家去。再一看两个小儿子穿的都是棉花絮的新棉衣。父亲难过得掉下眼泪。他责备自己让儿子忍冻干活，憎恨后妻虐待子骞。他不顾后妻下跪磕头求饶，执意要将她赶出家门。

子骞泪如雨下，苦苦哀求父亲道："母亲在家，就我一个人受寒；母亲要是走了，三个孩子都要受冻，望父亲大人深思啊！"

父亲感到儿子的话在理，便将后妻留下来。继母见子骞以德报怨，很受感动，从此对三个儿子一样对待。子骞长大后，孝名闻于天下。

孔子称赞说："闵子骞真是个孝子啊，他孝顺父母，友爱兄弟，让别人对他的父母兄弟都没有不好的闲话。"

【点评】

子骞孝母，闻名天下。以德报怨，世人传颂。

Ziqian Persuades His Father to Forgive His Stepmother

Min Ziqian was from the State of Lu during the Spring and Autumn Period. He was a student of Confucius.

His mother died when he was still very young. His father married another woman. Although very young, Ziqian was filled with filial piety for his parents. He always obediently served food to his parents and after they finished, he would clean up. Later his stepmother gave birth to two children. After that, Ziqian had a hard time. He was ordered around by his stepmother like a slave. In the daytime, he had to play with his brothers, and at night he had to talk his brothers to sleep. He was often beaten up whenever his stepmother felt dissatisfied.

On a cold day in winter, Ziqian was driving a cart for his father. Facing the chilly wind and snow, he was too cold to hold the reins tightly. His father scolded him for lack of attention and Ziqian kept silent. But he still could not hold the reins. Looking at his son's thick cotton-padded coat and thinking his son must have faked being cold, his father flew into a fury and used the whip to beat him. But his father was shocked to see that his padded clothes were stuffed with reed flowers instead of cotton. No wonder he felt cold. Wondering how his wife could do this, he returned home with Ziqian. When he saw his son's two brothers wearing new cotton-padded clothes, he felt very sad and tears came into his eyes. He blamed himself for having let his son work in the cold and hated that his wife mistreated his son. He was so angry that he decided to drive his wife away, despite his wife kneeling down and kowtowing for forgiveness.

Ziqian cried sadly. He begged his father not to do so, saying, "When my stepmother is at home, only I suffered from the cold; if she is driven away, the three will suffer. Father, please reconsider."

His father felt it was reasonable and gave up the idea. His stepmother was moved by Ziqian for his returning good for evil. From then on, she treated all three sons the same way. When Ziqian grew up, his filial piety was known all over the country.

The Master Confucius praised him, "Filial indeed is Ziqian! He loves his parents and brothers, which leaves no gossip for others to talk about his family."

【Comment】

Ziqian became well known far and wide for his filial piety to his stepmother. The story about his returning good for evil has been passed down from generation to generation.

子路负米孝亲

子路是春秋时期鲁国人，他身材高大，耿直豪爽，武艺高强，对父母十分孝顺，是乡里有名的孝子。

子路年轻时，因家境贫困，常去富贵人家干活。因他饭量大，时常以糠菜、杂粮充饥，但他从不让父母吃一顿糠菜。

有一次，子路听说陬邑有大米出售，而他父母正想吃米饭，但大米价格比杂粮要贵得多。为了使父母吃上大米，他就给寺庙修路，每天背石块上山。拿到了工钱后，走50里路上陬邑买米，背回家给父母烧白米饭。两老连声赞道："这大米饭真好吃呀！"子路听了心中十分高兴，但他自己则仍吃杂粮。

后来，子路拜孔子为师，由于他勤奋好学，长进很快，经常受到孔子的称赞。但孔子看到他每隔一月总要请假回家，认为他家庭观念太重，会影响学业。

一天，孔子问子路："你经常请假，是不是你父母有病？"子路回答说："老师，实不相瞒，我父母最爱吃大米饭，所以学生常要到陬邑背米。这是不能改变的，望老师原谅。"

孔子听了，对周围的学生说："子路真是一名大孝子呀！"

几位学生对子路说："你从家到陬邑来回100里，难道不辛苦吗?"

子路说道: "双亲年迈,能够给他们一点满足,表达做儿子的一番孝心,这是老师平日对我的教导。回家背米,既路远又辛苦,但只要想到老人能得到安慰,我就会精神百倍。"

子路的父母去世后不久,楚国请子路去做官。他有了百辆马车,还有100多担稻谷的俸禄,显贵一时。有一次,子路在用餐时,端起香喷喷的白米饭,对着酒肉菜肴,想到过去为父母负米的往事,感叹不已,就哼起了一首歌:

> 昔日百里负米,回家两老开颜;
> 现今父母去世,未能与我同席。
> 但愿草木不凋,无奈霜雪难熬;
> 正如鱼儿过河,对着流水而泣。
> 苍天如若见情,伴来亡灵共餐;
> 人寿终究有数,不孝后悔莫及。

歌罢,子路望着米饭佳肴久久不能下咽。

【点评】

子路负米孝双亲,做官不忘父母恩。一句"人寿终究有数,不孝后悔莫及",令天下儿女回味无穷。

Zi Lu Carries Rice
for His Parents

Zi Lu, from the State of Lu during the Spring and Autumn Period, was a big man. He was honest, excelled in martial arts, and was noted for his filial piety to his parents.

When he was young, the family was very poor, so he often worked for rich people. He ate a lot, but he would rather eat wild vegetables and coarse grain than let his parents do so.

Once, he heard that there was rice for sale in a marketplace called Zouyi. His parents wanted to have a taste of rice, but it was much more expensive than coarse grain. In order to let his parents eat rice, Zi Lu built roads for a temple and carried stones uphill every day to earn some money. With the money, he walked 25 kilometers to Zouyi to buy rice and finally carried it back home. His parents were very pleased to eat the rice, saying, "What delicious rice! " Hearing that, Zi Lu was very happy, but he himself ate only coarse grain.

Later on, he became a disciple of Confucius. He was diligent and a fast learner and often won praises from Confucius. But when Confucius found that he would ask for leave every other month, he thought Zi Lu focused too much on his family, which would affect his learning.

One day, Confucius asked Zi Lu "Is it because your parents are ill that you often ask for leave?" Zi Lu answered, "Master, as a matter of fact, my parents love rice. So I often go to Zouyi to buy rice for them. I cannot change this. Please forgive me."

Hearing this, Confucius said to his students, "What a great filial son Zi Lu is!"

Zi Lu's classmates asked him, "It is 50 kilometers from here to Zouyi. Isn't that laborious?"

Zi Lu replied, "Both of my parents are old. I will be very happy if I can do something to satisfy them and show my filial piety. This is also what our master teaches us. It is a hard and long way to carry the rice back, but when I see my parents comforted, my spirit soars."

Soon after his parents died, Zi Lu was invited to the State of Chu to be an official. He led a splendid life with 100 horse-drawn carriages at his disposal and more than 5000 kilograms of rice as his wages. Once, the white rice and meat on the table reminded him of the past when he carried rice for his parents, and a song came to his mind:

I traveled 50 kilometers to buy rice for my parents in the past,

Back at home I saw them full of smiles;

Now both of them have passed away,

Unable to feast together with me;

I wish wood and grass would never wither,

But frost and snow does come;

Just like fish swimming in the water,

They weep against the stream;

I wish heaven would witness all these,

And revive the dead souls to my dinner table;

Human life is limited,

And there will be endless regret if not filial to the old when they are alive.

Zi Lu finished singing, but he could hardly eat the delicacies.

【Comment】

Zi Lu carried rice for his parents when they were alive. Even after he became an official after his parents' death, he did not forget his parents. "Human life is limited, and there will be endless regret if not filial to the old when they are alive." This should well serve as a reminder for all sons and daughters in the world.

张良敬老得兵书

　　张良原是战国时韩国的贵公子，后韩国被秦灭亡，他雇了个大力士去博浪沙（今河南原阳县东南）刺杀秦始皇，事败后，他流落到下邳（今江苏睢宁北），更改姓名，在当地隐藏起来。

　　有一天，张良路过沂水旁的一座石桥，看到桥上坐着一位穿着粗布衣服的老人，鹤发童颜，神态飘逸。心想这老人决非凡人，就走上去与他攀谈。忽然，那老人将脚一扬，把一只鞋子甩到桥下，对他说："小伙子，把那只鞋替我捡起来！"

　　张良见这老人如此无礼，真想给他吃一拳头，可看到老人一蓬白须，一副老态龙钟的模样，就忍着气把鞋子捡起送到他面前。

　　"小伙子，把鞋帮我穿上！"老人伸出脚，悠然地说。

　　张良觉得又好气又好笑，心想：索性好人做到底吧，随即跪下，帮老人穿上了鞋。

　　老人看看张良，笑了笑，也不道谢，转身走去。张良觉得好奇，就暗暗跟着老人走了一里路。那老人回头对张良说："孺子可教，五日后清早，再与我在桥上见面。"

　　张良觉得这位老人绝非平庸之辈，就拱手回答："五日后再见。"

第五日清早，张良到桥下，哪知老人已在桥上候他了。他还没走到桥上，老人就生气地说："五日后早点来吧!"说完扶杖而去。

约定的时间又到了。这次张良和衣稍歇，半夜起身到了桥上，等到东方鱼白时老人也来了。那老人见张良敬老心诚，喜滋滋地说："你有如此诚心，将来定可干一番大事。"说着从怀里取出一部书来送给张良，并叮嘱道："你熟读此书，就可辅助明君夺取天下，10年后必成大业。"

张良立即跪下接过这部书，正想说些感谢的话，只见老人已飘然而去。这位老人就是有名的黄石公。

张良回来打开那本书，见是姜尚写的《太公兵法》，书上还有黄石公的许多批注。心想：此书自秦始皇焚书坑儒以来已成旷世之宝，加上黄石公的精心批注，更是宝中之宝。

从此，张良日夜研读这部《太公兵法》。10年后，陈涉起兵抗秦，张良也随之准备起义。后在刘邦帐下成为一位重臣，为汉高祖统一天下立下了汗马功劳。

【点评】

老年人是财富。敬老积德，敬老受益。

Zhang Liang Receives a Book on the Art of Warfare for Respecting his Elders

Zhang Liang was a son of a rich family of the State of Han during the Warring States Period. Later, the State of Han was conquered by Qin. Zhang Liang hired a strong man to assassinate the first Emperor of the Qin Dynasty, but it failed. Zhang went into hiding in Xiapi (now north of Suining of Jiangsu Province) under another name.

One day, when he passed over a stone bridge by the Yi River, Zhang saw an old man sitting on the bridge. He was wearing coarse cloth and had grey hair, but he had a child's face, looking relaxed and graceful. Zhang thought him quite extraordinary, so he went up to talk with him. Suddenly, the old man lifted one of his feet, and his shoe fell into the water under the bridge. "Young man, go and get me my shoe!" The old man ordered. Zhang felt that the old man was very impolite and wanted to hit him, but withdrew seeing his grey beard and old appearance. Calming his anger, he went under the bridge and brought back the shoe for the old man.

"Young man, put it on for me! " The old man stretched out his foot.

Zhang felt both angry and slightly amused. He thought, all right, let me just be good to you till the very end. Then he knelt down and put the shoe on for the old man.

Glancing at Zhang Liang, the old man smiled and turned away, without saying even a word of thanks. Zhang Liang felt it strange, so he stealthily followed the old man for a while. The old man suddenly turned back and said, "You are teachable. Meet me on the bridge in five days."

Zhang was sure that this old man was by no means an ordinary man, so he saluted him and answered, "See you in five days."

On the morning of the fifth day, Zhang Liang came to the bridge and saw the old man already waiting there. Hardly had he climbed the bridge when the old man said angrily, "Come earlier in another five days! " Then he left.

The appointed time came. Afraid of being late again, Zhang got up at midnight and came to the bridge. When dawn came, the old man arrived. Full of smiles, the old man said, "You are so determined and sincere that you will have something big to accomplish." With these words, the old man took out a book from under his clothes and said, "Read this book carefully. One

中华敬老故事精选

day you will help your master conquer the world. You will ac-complish something great in ten years."

Zhang Liang knelt down right away and took the book re-spectfully. But before he could say thank you, the old man was already gone. This old man was actually the famous Huang Shigong.

Opening the book, Zhang Liang found that it was a book on the Art of Warfare written by Jiang Shang and there were many notes added by Huang Shigong. Zhang said to himself, "This became a rare book after the emperor of the Qin burned a lot of books and buried many Confucian scholars alive to control his country. With Huang Shigong's notes, this book is a remarkable treasure."

After that, he studied the book day and night. Ten years later, when Chen She rose against the Qin, Zhang Liang also started an uprising. Later on, he became an important official under Liu Bang and achieved notable merits in helping Liu Bang unify the country.

【Comment】

Our elders are wealth. By respecting the elderly and treating them with virtue, one will benefit much.

中华敬老故事精选

Selected China Stories of Elder-Respecting

韩信报恩浣衣妇

　　韩信是汉高祖手下的一名大将。他出身于江苏淮阴一个穷苦的家庭，5岁时死了父亲，靠母亲给人洗衣缝补度日。17岁时，母亲因病去世，韩信无家可归，便到熟人家混碗饭吃，日子一长，人家就给他白眼看，他只得到处流浪。他没有手艺，又没有本钱做买卖，怎么办？后来他想出一个办法：到河边去钓鱼，以卖鱼谋生。

　　头几天，他还能每天钓上几条鱼，卖几个钱填饱肚子。后来河里鱼越来越少，他钓不到鱼，只好饿肚子。

　　一天，他从清早到晌午一条鱼都没钓上，肚子叽里咕噜直叫。在河边洗衣的一位大娘见他一副愁眉苦脸的模样，便拿出一块饭团分给他吃。一连十几天，大娘总是分给他一点饭团，韩信感到十分不好意思，对她说："我天天吃您的饭，您真是我的重生母亲，将来我一定要好好报答您老人家！"

　　大娘笑了笑对韩信说："我是看你可怜，才帮助你，谁要你来报答什么呢？"

　　韩信听了簌簌地流下了眼泪，向大娘磕了头，就离去了。

　　从此，韩信再也不钓鱼了，他到铁铺去打工，后来到刘邦军营里去当兵。在军营里，他白天习武练操，晚上苦读兵书。一次，他结识刘邦手下的谋臣萧何，两人谈论争天下之道和用兵之法，深得萧何器重。萧何向刘邦推荐他为大将。此后，他为汉王刘邦屡立战功，把项羽围困于垓下。刘邦打败项羽后封韩信为楚王。

韩信想到自己有今日的荣华富贵全靠过去那位大娘的哺饭之恩，就回到江苏老家去寻找那位大娘。

大娘已是满头白发，两眼昏花。韩信见了连忙双膝跪下："大娘，您还认得我钓鱼的韩信吗？"

大娘先是一惊，后来才想起来，说道："你就是韩信啊！"

"大娘，您是一位好心肠的老人，是我重生之母，我说过要报答您。"说完，韩信叫手下取出一千两黄金，他恭恭敬敬地送给了老大娘。

【点评】

知恩必报真君子，有恩不报是小人。

Han Xin Repays the Kindness of a Washing Woman

Han Xin was a great general under Emperor Han Gao Zu of the Han Dynasty. He was born to a poor family in Huaiyin of Jiangsu Province. His father died when he was five and his mother supported the family by washing clothes and doing needlework for others. Unfortunately, when Han was 17, his mother died of disease. Homeless, Han Xin went to his friends for meals. After a while, he was often given a cold shoulder and had to roam around. He had no skills and money for business, but he did manage to think of an idea to go fishing by the river and make a living by selling fish.

At the beginning he could fill his stomach by selling some fish. But later, there were fewer fish in the river, and he had to go without food.

One day, Han went fishing again. From early morning to late afternoon he got nothing, and his stomach started to rumble. A woman who was doing washing by the riverside saw him and gave him some food to eat. For days on end, the woman always let him share some rice balls.   Han Xin felt quite embarrassed. "You are really like my mother to give me food every day, and I will repay you for your kindness." Han said.

The woman said with a smile, "what I've done is out of pity, and I never expect you to repay anything."

Hearing this, Han Xin kowtowed to the woman, tears in his eyes, and left.

From then on, Han Xin stopped fishing.   He went to a blacksmith to do odd jobs for him and later joined Liu Bang's army.   In the army camp, he learned military skills in the day-time and read military books at night. Once, he talked about the art of war with Xiao He, a mastermind of Liu Bang and won good praises from him.   Xiao He recommended him to Liu Bang, who appointed him a general. After that, Han won many victories in battles against Xiang Yu.   Liu Bang defeated Xiang Yu finally and he made Han Xin the King of Chu.

As a king, Han Xin thought of the woman who gave him food and his present wealth and honor, so he returned to Jiangsu to look for her.

Seeing the dim-sighted woman with grey hair, Han Xin hur-riedly knelt down in front of her, "Aunt, do you recognize me, Han Xin, who did the fishing? "

The woman was startled at first, but then remembered, "Yes, you are Han Xin! "

"Aunt, you were as kind to me as my mother.   I said I would repay you."   Han Xin took out 1000 taels of gold and presented them to the old woman with his full respect.

【Comment】

It is a real gentleman who repays the debt of gratitude; and it is a small man who does not.

司马迁不负父命

在一间阴森森的囚牢里，一个手脚戴着刑具的犯人蜷缩在刑房的角落里。这个犯人就是辉煌巨著《史记》的作者司马迁。3年前，父亲司马谈去世，他继承父职，在汉武帝手下任太史令。

一天，汉武帝问他对李陵在与匈奴作战中投降一事的看法。司马迁从李陵平时的为人以及当时敌强我弱的形势加以分析，认为李陵是有功之臣，他的投降实属无奈，将来必为朝廷效命。汉武帝听罢心中大怒，以"欺君罔上"之罪，把他投入监狱，并判处死刑。

这场自天而降的横祸使司马迁悲愤至极。他在牢中凝视着窗外的月光，回想起生前的父亲。

司马迁10岁时，父亲带他到家乡陕西韩城郊外河边，只见奔腾咆哮的黄河向龙门山滚滚冲击。父亲给他讲了一个古代的传说："每年都有千千万万条鲤鱼逆流而上，想穿过龙门山后化为神龙上天，可是那些意志薄弱的鲤鱼都触山而死，只有毫不灰心、坚忍不拔的72条鲤鱼跃过龙门，成为火眼金爪的巨龙，直向天门飞去……"

公元前110年，司马迁出使西南巴蜀回家时，父亲已病入膏肓。他跪在父亲的病榻旁给父亲端上了一碗汤药，父亲摆摆手，对他说："我死之后，你要接替我的位置，继承祖先的事业。自从孔子死后，至今400多年了，没有一部像样的史书。我身为太史，没能做成这件事，真担心天下的史籍文化从此断绝，你要记住我的话，写成一部《史记》……"

司马迁泪流满面，哭泣着说："儿虽不敏，但一定记住完成父亲未完成的事业，把《史记》写出来。"

狱中的司马迁想到这里，站起身来，两手紧紧攥住窗棂，口中喃喃地说："父亲，我不会忘记你的遗训……我一定要活下来！"

按照汉代的律法，死囚可花大钱赎罪，但司马迁拿不出那么多钱；剩下的办法是接受宫刑，这是对人格的极大侮辱。想到这里，他心中一阵寒噤：这种肉体和精神的痛苦简直比慷慨引决还要难受百倍啊！但是，为了继承父亲的大业，他决心忍受一切痛苦。

第二天，司马迁通知狱司转告汉武帝：他愿意接受宫刑。

司马迁被释放后，开始发奋写作，每天写到深夜。汉武帝征和二年（公元前91年），司马迁终于完成了共130卷、53万字的巨著《史记》。

【点评】

为了成就伟大事业，必须付出巨大代价。司马迁不负父命，忍辱著史的故事，给人深刻启迪。

Sima Qian Lives up to His Father's Expectations

In a dark and gloomy prison cell, an inmate was huddling in a corner. He was none other than Sima Qian, the author of the monumental works Records of the Historian. Three years before, he inherited his father's position of Tai Shi, an imperial official in charge of compiling historical documentations, and he worked under the Han emperor Han Wu Di.

One day, the emperor asked for his opinion about the Han general Li Ling's surrender in a battle with Xiong Nu, the Huns. Judging by Li Ling's behavior and the battle situation, Sima Qian thought that Li Ling was a general with good performance, and that he could not help but surrender in the face of a much stronger enemy in battle. He was sure to loyally serve the imperial court in the future. The Han emperor was furious to hear the opinion and threw Sima Qian into prison for disrespecting the emperor and sentenced him to death.

Sima Qian fell into grief and indignation because of the unexpected disaster. Looking at the moonlight outside the small window of the prison cell, Sima Qian recalled a story his father told him.

His father took him to the Yellow River in the rural area of Han City of Shaanxi Province when he was 10. They saw the waves of roaring water pounding the Dragon Gate Mountain. His father told him an ancient legend: "Thousands of carp swam upstream every year, attempting to cross the Dragon Gate in the hope of becoming dragons and going up to the sky. All the weak-willed carp died after bumping against the mountain. Only 72 carp that were not downhearted jumped over the Dragon Gate and became giant dragons with fiery eyes and golden paws, flying up to the sky."

In 110 BC, when Sima Qian came back from Sichuan after a court mission, his father was incurably ill. He knelt down by his father's bed and served his father his medicine. Waving his hand, his father said, "When I die, you need to inherit my position to complete the family cause. Since the death of Confucius 400 years ago, there hasn't been a single well-compiled history book. As a court historian, I didn't finish my job. I was worried that such cultural history would be lost. You should follow my will and finish a history book."

Sima Qian, his face covered with tears, answered, "I am not smart, but I promise to continue your cause and finish this book."

Thinking of all this, Sima Qian stood up and clenched the prison window bars, saying to himself, "Father, I will live on and carry your will through to the end! "

Han laws allowed prisoners to atone for their crimes with a large sum of money. But Sima Qian couldn't afford this, so he only had one second choice—castration, which was a huge indignity. Thinking of this, he shivered. The physical and mental pain was hundreds of times worse than dying with dignity! However, for the sake of his father's will, he was determined to endure all the sufferings in the prison.

The next day Sima Qian told the prison official that he made his choice.

After he was released, he began to write day and night. During the second year of the reign of the emperor (in 91 BC), he finally completed the great works, Records of the Historian, 130 volumes, with over 530,000 Chinese characters.

【Comment】

To accomplish a great cause, it is necessary to sacrifice greatly. Sima Qian lived up to the expectations of his father and swallowed up all humiliation to record history. The story is profoundly educating.

蔡文姬为父续书

蔡邕是东汉末年的名士，他学识渊博，精通经史、音律、天文，又以文章、诗赋、篆刻、书法盛名于世。豪强董卓专权时，为笼络人心，请他出来做官，对他十分敬重。三天连升三级。后董卓被王允所杀，蔡邕从此不得志。

蔡邕有个女儿，取字文姬。她从小聪明伶俐，因受父亲影响，十几岁时就通琴棋诗书。

一次，她听到父亲在书房里弹琴时断弦，就走出来说："父亲，你的琴第二根弦断了吧！"父亲以为她偶尔猜中，待她离去后故意将第三根弦拨断，又问女儿，文姬回答得一点不错。从此，蔡邕把她视作掌上明珠，亲自教她诗文、音律，有时父女俩一起作诗唱和。

文姬不仅敬重父亲，而且十分孝顺。父亲写字，她在旁研墨；父亲有病，她煎烧汤药，日夜侍奉在侧。

文姬长大后，嫁给河南卫仲道为妻。不久，丈夫病死，她就回家守寡。父亲死后，母亲因过度悲伤，也跟着去世了。从此，蔡文姬孤身一人回到故乡陈留，一心整理父亲的著作。

董卓死后又发生李傕、郭汜的混战，长安一带百姓到处逃难，蔡文姬也跟着难民流亡。一次，她在途中被一支趁火打劫的匈奴兵掳走献给左贤王。左贤王见她美貌多才，十分怜爱，纳她为妃子。

蔡文姬忍辱含屈在匈奴住了12年，好在左贤王对她十分体贴，又生下了一男一女。但她仍日夜缅怀父亲和中原故国，经常对月弹琴，用琴声寄托对父亲的思念之情。

公元216年，曹操统一了北方，在邺城当了丞相，封为魏王。他想起了10多年前的故友蔡邕，并得知蔡文姬在匈奴的消息，便派董祀为使节，带着大批金银财宝去赎蔡文姬归汉。

蔡文姬听得曹丞相派人来接她回中原，心中十分矛盾。返回故国是她日日夜夜的梦想，但又不忍离开两个子女，就央求左贤王让她把孩子带走，即使带回一个也行。

左贤王说："曹丞相派使者要你回去整理你父亲的遗著，单于已经同意了，我只得遵命，但孩子是匈奴人，我决不能让你带走。"

为了实现父亲生前的遗愿，蔡文姬忍痛离开一对心爱的孩子，随着董祀走了。

到达长安郊外父亲的墓地时，蔡文姬长跪在墓前失声痛哭，又弹唱了自编的《胡笳十八拍》。歌词中寄托了她缅怀父亲养育之恩的深情，抒发了自己在与百姓颠沛流离中的哀伤，在旁的董祀听了潸然泪下。蔡文姬对董祀说："父亲早年得罪了宦官，被流放到朔方；逃出了厄运回到洛阳后，我们父女俩相依为命。我失去了丈夫后又失去了父母，在战乱中流落匈奴，我一生的命运与父亲一样悲苦。这次回到中原，我一定要遵从父亲的遗愿整理他的遗稿，否则我就成为世上不孝的女儿了！"

蔡文姬到了邺城，曹操为她与董祀完婚，还送给他们一所房子和两名奴婢。一天，蔡文姬前来答谢曹操，曹操问她：

"听说夫人家有不少蔡邕先生的书籍文稿，现在还保存着吗?"

蔡文姬叹了口气说："家父生前留下4000多卷书，可惜几经大乱，全都散失了，不过我还能背出400多卷来。"

曹操听得她能背出那么多，高兴地说："夫人真是一代才女! 你要把它写出来，这可是一笔珍贵的财富啊!"后来，蔡文姬在家中悬挂起父亲的画像，花了几年时间，把她所能记住的几百篇父亲的文章默写出来，还续写了《后汉书》，实现了父亲的遗愿。

【点评】

一曲《胡笳十八拍》，涌流出一生悲苦和思父情怀。如果不是父女情深，怎能背写出400多卷遗书? 蔡文姬为父续书的故事感人至深。

Cai Wenji Completes
Her Father's Works

Cai Yong, a famous scholar in the late Eastern Han Dynasty, was proficient in philosophical writings and literature, musical temperament and astronomy. He was also well known for his articles, poems, seal cutting and calligraphy. During the time that the tyrant Dong Zhuo had power over the country, Dong Zhuo invited Cai Yong to be an official in order to win over the people's support. He respected Cai Yong and promoted his official rank three times within three days. After Dong Zhuo was killed by Wang Yun, Cai Yong was ignored.

Cai Yong had a daughter, called Cai Wenji. She was very intelligent and, under her father's influence, was very skilled in playing the lyre, playing chess, and writing poems and calligraphy when she was only in her teens.

Once, she heard her father playing the qin (a seven-stringed plucked instrument similar to the zither) in his study and heard a broken string. She went to her father and asked, "Father, is the second string broken? " Thinking his daughter just made a lucky guess, he snapped the third string on purpose when she was leaving and asked her to guess. Wenji was right again. From then on, Cai Yong saw his daughter as a pearl in his palm. He taught her himself poems and musical temperament. Sometimes they would write poems and sing together.

Wenji was respectful and filial to her father. When her father was writing, she would attend to him by making ink; when he was ill, she would boil medicine for him and serve him day and night.

Cai Wenji later married a man called Wei Zhongdao from Henan. Soon he died of disease. Following his untimely death, she returned to her father's house as a widow. Her father died later, and her mother died of grieving. Then Wenji went back to her hometown, Chenliu, alone and sorted out her father's writings.

After the tyrant Dong Zhuo died, two generals, Li Jue and Guo Si, fought against each other for power, which brought panic to the people in the capital Chang'an. Wenji followed the refugees, and on the way she was taken away by Xiong Nu soldiers, who had entered the capital. Wenji was brought to the Left Crown King, who admired her beauty and brightness and took her as his concubine.

Wenji endured all the disgrace and stayed in Xiong Nu for 12 years. Fortunately the king treated her well, and she bore two children, one boy and one girl. She missed her father and her own country very much. She would play the qin in the moonlight and place her thoughts in the music.

In 216 AD, Cao Cao unified the north of China and became a prime minister in the City of Ye, with the title King of Wei. He thought of his old friend Cai Yong and heard about his daughter Wenji. He sent Dong Si as his envoy with a lot of treasure to ransom Wenji.

When Wenji heard about this, she felt herself in a dilemma. She dreamed about returning to her country, but on the other hand she didn't want to leave her children. So she begged the Left Crown King to allow her to take her children with her, even just one of them.

The king said, "Prime Minister Cao wanted you back to sort out your father's writings and Chan Yu (the Xiong Nu chief) has agreed. I must respect this. But your children are Huns, so I cannot let you take them."

To fulfill her father's will, Wenji had to leave her beloved children and came back with the envoy.

She came to Chang'an and paid homage to her father in front of his grave. She knelt down, crying bitterly and played her own works, Eighteen Songs of a Nomad Flute, to express her profound sentiments to her father and her sufferings during her captivity. Seeing this, the envoy Dong Si shed tears silently. Wenji said to Dong Si, "My father was exiled to the north for having offended a eunuch. After he came back to Luoyang, we depended on each other. I lost my husband, and then my parents, and I was stranded in Xiong Nu. I had a sad and bitter life as my father did. Now that I have come home, I am determined to sort out my father's writings; otherwise I will be an unfilial daughter to my father！"

Then Cai Wenji returned to the City of Ye, where Cao Cao arranged her marriage with Dong Si and gave her a house and two maid-servants. One day Cai Wenji went to thank Cao Cao. Cao Cao asked, "I was told you kept a lot of your father's writings at home. Do you still have them？"

Wenji sighed, saying, "My father left about 4000 volumes of works, but after the war, most of them were lost. However, I could still recall over 400 volumes from memory."

Cao Cao was very happy to hear that she could still recite that many. "What a talented woman you are！ If you can write them down, you will leave us a precious treasure." Later, Cai Wenji hung her father's portrait at home and spent several years recording all she could remember of her father's works. She also extended the book History of Late Han and fulfilled her father's will.

【Comment】

The tune of Eighteen Songs of a Nomad Flute tells her sufferings and her yearning for her father. If not for the profound bond between them, how could she recall most of the several hundred works of her father? The story is indeed moving.

李密尽孝辞诏书

魏、蜀、吴被灭之后，西晋取而代之。这时，备受诸葛亮赏识的蜀汉小吏李密受到当朝器重。什么原因呢？据说此人一有才学，二能尽孝。因此，李密所在犍为郡的太守一眼看中了他，竭力向上面举荐。之后，益州刺史又卖力推举，但都被李密谢绝。他们问："为何不从？"李密道："祖母无人照料。"不久，此事传到晋武帝司马炎的耳朵里，为笼络蜀国旧臣，他特例下了诏书，可李密依然拒不从命。这下惹怒了武帝，认为李密故意逃避，不把皇帝放在眼里。

李密心中十分矛盾，如若遵诏前往，祖母的病情会一天天加重；想保全祖母，报养育之恩，而皇上又不答应，怎么办呢？李密忽然想到：武帝以孝治天下，如果我将实情详细禀告，也许会得到他的宽容。

于是，李密蘸墨挥毫，以满腹辛酸泪写了一篇《陈情表》，内容大致如下：

"我是个多灾多难的人，母亲生下我才6个月，刚刚会笑的时候慈爱的父亲就死了。到我4岁的时候，可恶的舅舅强迫我母亲改嫁。从此，我痛失双亲，连做梦也在呼喊爹娘呀！尔后，我被病魔折腾得死去活来，9岁了还不会走路。其间，我每吃一顿饭、喝一碗药水、洗补一件衣服靠谁呢？只有我敬爱的老祖母。人有近亲，可我伯叔、兄弟全无；门外门里，冷冷清清，只有我祖孙二人相依为命。"

"陛下，承蒙您恩赐，提拔我为洗马，这是我以前做梦也没有想到的呀，应该好好侍奉太子。您的大恩大德，即使我用生命也难以报答；何况我是亡国之俘，十分浅陋低下。您过高地看中我，优待我，哪里敢犹豫而有所奢望呢？只是因为祖母老病兼袭，气息奄奄，朝不保夕。"

"陛下，我孤苦异常，若没有祖母的抚养，就没法活到今天；祖母年迈力衰，多病缠身，如果我不伺候，就无人养老送终。我今年44岁，祖母今年96岁。我伺候祖母的时间不多了，可报效陛下的日子还很长呢。所以，恳请您洞察我的苦楚，同意我暂不赴任，日后当尽犬马之劳。"

武帝看完信，眼眶湿润了，低声连连称道："好孝孙！好孝孙！"同意了李密伺候祖母、日后赴任的请求。

（文　李天佑）

【点评】

李密的一篇《陈情表》，不仅打动了晋武帝，更打动了世世代代的中国百姓，成为中国知识分子做人和作文的典范。

Li Mi Turns Down an Imperial Offer

For the Sake of His Ailing Grandmother

After the time of the three kingdoms Wei, Shu and Wu was over, the Western Jin took over. At that time Li Mi, a low-ranking official from Shu, was appreciated by Zhuge Liang, the very intelligent Prime Minister of Shu, and was a knowledgeable man in the Western Jin Dynasty. Li Mi was not only a learned man, but also known for his filial piety. The chief of the local county thought highly of him and tried to recommend him to his superiors. Later the governor of Yizhou recommended him to the court again. Li Mi turned them both down. They asked, "Why won't you take the position?" "I need to take care of my grand-ma," Li answered. Soon the story spread to the ears of Sima Yan, the emperor of the Western Jin. To win over some officials' support who had worked for the Kingdom of Shu in the past, he issued an imperial edict especially to him. But Li Mi refused. This made the emperor angry. He presumed that Li Mi was trying to purposely avoid him and disrespect even the emperor. Li Mi found himself in a dilemma. If he took the position, no one could take care of his grandma and her physical condition would get worse. If he refused the position again to stay and take care of his grandma, the emperor would not agree. Believing that the emperor was known for governing the country with filial piety, Li Mi decided to write a statement to tell the emperor about his family situation in the hope of being forgiven.

Li Mi wrote the statement full of sadness and bitterness, which read:

I'm a man with bitter experiences. When I was only 6 months old and had just learned how to smile, my kind father died. When I was 4, my vicious uncle forced my mother to re-marry. Since then I lost both of my dear parents. I called for my parents even in my dreams. Then I was so tormented by disease that I still didn't know how to walk at the age of 9. I could only depend on my grandma for every meal, every bowl of medicine and every piece of clean clothes. Everyone but me has close relatives. In the whole family, there is only my grandmother and me, depending on each other.

Your Majesty, I feel very honored that you would promote me to Xi Ma (an official title of high ranking). This is something I have never dreamed of, and it is my duty to serve the princes. I could never repay your benevolence, even with my life. I am just a normal citizen from a conquered kingdom, with inferior position. You have too high an expectation of me and offer very good treatment. I couldn't expect it to be better. I cannot take it on—

ly because my grandmother is advanced in age and is on the verge of death for serious illness.

Your majesty, I am extraordinary in loneliness and suffering. Without my grandmother, I could never have lived until today. Now she is old and ill, no one can attend to her except me. I am 44 and my grandmother is 96. It will not be long for me to care for her. But the days will be long for me to devote my life to your majesty. May you discern my misery and allow me to refuse the offer temporarily. I will do everything I can to repay your kindness.

After reading the statement, the Emperor of Wu, with tears in his eyes, acclaimed repeatedly, "What a great grandson with filial piety!" and gave his nod to his pleading.

（Li Tianyou）

【Comment】

Li Mi's personal statement moved not only Emperor Wu of the Western Jin Dynasty but also the common people of generations. It has become a model for Chinese intellectuals to learn to be people of integrity and for students in writing compositions.

王羲之和水饺师傅

晋代大书法家王羲之被称为"书圣",他的儿子王献之也是一位大书法家,人称"二王"。

王献之自幼跟父亲学书法,7岁时他对父亲说:"我的字再写3年也就行了吧?"王羲之对他说:"你能写完18大缸的水,你的字才能站稳脚跟。"3年后,王羲之见儿子的书艺有了进步,但见他开始自满,心中十分担心。有一次,王献之和同学举行一场书法观摩会,请王羲之到会评判。会后,这批少年问王羲之:"先生年轻时曾拜何人为师?"

"我最初有两位老师,第一位是我的母亲,叫卫夫人,你们都知道。第二位老师是做饺子的女师傅。"王羲之说着向众人讲了一段故事。

王羲之17岁时在母亲卫夫人的指点下书艺大有长进,笔锋初露,震惊了方圆百里,许多人赶来请他题字、写对联。王羲之少年得志,有些飘飘然起来。

一天,他经过一家饺子铺,看见门楣上写着"鸭儿饺子铺",门的两边写着:"经此过不去,知味且常来。"王羲之看到这10个大字写得毫无骨力,结构又差劲,心想:是谁写出这种字来献丑？正想转过身去，腹中感到饥饿，又见铺内食客满座，就走了进去。

王羲之见矮墙边有一口大锅，锅内沸水翻滚。只见一只只饺子从墙上飞来，不偏不倚只只都落入锅的中央，十分准确。他看得惊呆了。

王羲之坐下招呼伙计，不久伙计端上一大盘水饺，只见个个水饺玲珑精巧，活像浮在水面的游鸭。再尝尝饺子，鲜美可口，不一会儿他便把一盘水饺吃下肚去。

付账后，王羲之问店主在哪里，伙计指了指矮墙那边。他看见一位白发老太坐在一块大面板前独自擀饺子皮，包饺子馅，动作利索娴熟，不一会儿一批饺子包好。只见她一边与伙计讲话，一边随手把一只只饺子抛出墙外，连看都不看一眼。

王羲之惊叹不已，欠身问道："敢问老妈妈，你学了几年才练成了这手功夫？"

"熟则50年，深练要一生。"白发老太回答说。

王羲之听了，心想，自己学写字不过十几年就自满起来，好不应该，不觉脸上一阵发热。

"吃了贵店的饺子果然名不虚传，但门口的对联为什么不请人写得好一点？"

那老太一听生气地说："你这位相公有所不知，我何尝不想请名人写副对子，只是像王羲之那种人架子太大，学了不到我这功夫的一半时间就眼睛抬上脑门，哪里会瞧得起我这店铺？我看他的那点功夫还比不上我这扔饺子功夫的一半深呢！"说完只顾做饺子，连看也不看王羲之一眼。

王羲之听了这番话，一时面红耳赤。

第二天，他亲自把给饺子铺写好的一副对联送到白发老太手中。白发老太受了这副对子，见来人便是王羲之，不好意思地说："昨天不知王相公到来，言语失敬了，还请王相公原谅！"

王羲之回答说："师傅给学生讲的一番话，真是胜读10年书啊！您老就是我的师父，请受学生一拜。"

此后，王羲之格外虚心刻苦练习，把水饺老太讲的话当作座右铭，终于成为一代"书圣"。

【点评】

每个老人都是一部书。尊敬老人，虚心求教，就能获得个中真谛。

Wang Xizhi and the Dumpling Maker

Wang Xizhi, the great calligrapher of the Jin Dynasty, was known as a "calligraphy sage." His son Wang Xianzhi was a calligrapher as well and together with his father they were called the "Two Wangs."

Wang Xianzhi learned calligraphy from his father since he was a small boy. When he was 7, he asked his father, "Will I be good enough if I practice for three more years?" His father answered, "When you use up all the water from the 18 big pots, it is time." Three years later, Wang Xizhi saw his son's great progress in calligraphy, but felt worried, seeing that his son had become self-satisfied. Once, Wang Xianzhi and his classmates held a calligraphy exhibition. They invited Wang Xizhi as a judge. After the exhibition, the students asked Wang Xizhi, "Who taught you when you were young?"

"I had two teachers. One was my mother Mrs. Wei. You all knew her. The other one was a female dumpling-making master, " Wang Xizhi said, and started to tell a story.

Under the tutoring of his mother, 17-year-old Wang Xizhi made big progress in calligraphy, and he was well known far and wide. Many people came to him for writing inscriptions and couplets. He felt very proud of himself and became self-satisfied.

One day, when he was passing a dumpling house called Duckling Dumpling, he saw a couplet on both sides of the door, reading "Don't pass here with haste; Come back after you taste", and he regarded the writing as very poor. Ready to leave, he suddenly felt a little hungry, so he stepped into the house.

Wang saw a big boiling pot by a wall and dumplings flew down from over the wall accurately into the center of the pot. He was startled to see this.

He then sat down by a table and a plate of dumplings was served. The dumplings were exquisitely made, just like small ducklings swimming in water. He tasted and found it very delicious. In a moment, he finished them all.

He paid and asked to see the owner. The waiter pointed at the short wall. He saw a grey-haired woman sitting in front of a big plate kneading the dough and making dumplings in nimble movements. She threw the dumplings one by one over the wall into the boiling pot without even looking at it, while talking with other workers at the same time.

Surprised, Wang came up and bowed to ask, "How long did it take you to become so skillful? "

"It takes 50 years to become skillful and a whole life to become an expert." She answered.

Hearing this, Wang felt a bit ashamed for becoming arrogant after only a dozen years of practice.

"Your dumplings taste really good. But why don't you ask someone to write a better couplet? " Wang asked.

"You do not know." the woman was a little angry. "I did want to ask someone famous to write it, but people like Wang Xizhi were too arrogant to write it for this small restaurant. The time he spent practicing writing was no more than half the time I spent on my dumplings, but he felt quite conceited. But to me, his skill is not nearly half as proficient as mine." She did not even glance at Wang, but kept on making the dumplings.

Wang Xizhi felt his face and ears turning red.

The next day, he wrote a couplet and presented it to the grey-haired woman. Taking the couplet, the woman learned that the man was Wang Xizhi and apologized, "I didn't know it was you yesterday, so I had a slip of the tongue. Please forgive me."

But Wang said, "What you said to me is equivalent to my reading for ten years. You are my master and please accept my kowtow as your student."

From then on, Wang Xizhi worked even harder with his calligraphy and took the words of that grey-haired old woman as his motto. In the end he became the "sage of calligraphy."

【Comment】

Every elder is a book. Respecting our elders and learning modestly from them will help one learn the true meaning of life.

顾恺之为母画像

顾恺之是东晋大画家。他善于画人物，特别擅长画女人和神女，在画脸部时以点睛之笔使神情风采惟妙惟肖。他之所以特别擅长画女人，与他一片至诚的孝心有关。

顾恺之一出生，母亲就去世了，一直由奶奶带养。幼年的顾恺之，生得虎头虎脑，家人都叫他小虎子。他父亲曾是朝廷官员，因不满时政的黑暗腐败，退隐居家写诗著文。顾恺之常常冲进书房里问父亲："人家都有母亲我的母亲在哪儿？"

"虎子，你母亲到很远很远的外婆家去了。"父亲怕孩子难过，只好骗他。

"那母亲什么时候回来？"顾恺之睁着大眼又问。

"大概半年吧。。"

从此，顾恺之板着手指一日一日地等待母亲回家。半年后，他又去问父亲。父亲见瞒他不住，只好对孩子讲母亲去世的经过。

顾恺之得知自己生母已不在人世，不禁号啕大哭。父亲劝他说："孩子，人死不能复生，你以后不要再想母亲了。"

从此，顾恺之变得沉默寡言，心中只是想着母亲生得什么模样。他一次又一次询问父亲：母亲的脸长得啥样，身材长得啥样。父亲给他描述了一番后，他又去询问奶奶，一遍又一遍地听大人讲述后，他心中似乎有了母亲的形象。

8岁时，他对父亲说："我要给母亲画像。"

父亲摇摇头说："你没见过母亲，怎能画像？画出来也不会像的。"

顾恺之听了并没有灰心，他专心致志地学着画母亲，画完一张就去给父亲看，问画得像不像。

"不像，画得一点也不像。"父亲摇摇头。

顾恺之听了又接着画第二张，父亲又说画得不像，他又画。当画到第十张时，父亲说："身材手足有点像，面部不像。"

顾恺之听了好比吃了一杯蜜糖，心里甜滋滋的。他想：我终有一天能看到母亲的像。他花了半年功夫，画成一张母亲的全身画像拿给奶奶看。奶奶心疼孙子画得这么累，便对他说："真像你母亲，虎子你别再画了。"

顾恺之还不相信，再给父亲看。父亲连连点头说："像了，像了，只是眼神不太像。"

顾恺之从此天天专门学习画人物的眼睛，画了又改，改了又画。当他又把一张母亲的画像送到父亲书房里时，父亲一愣：这不是妻子出现在眼前了吗？忙说："这真是你的母亲，把这幅画挂起来吧！"

顾恺之到20岁时已成为卓越的肖像画家。当同行们问他曾拜谁为老师时，顾恺之说："我的母亲是我心中一直活着的老师。"

【点评】

精诚所至，金石为开。顾恺之凭着一颗拳拳思母之心，成为一位卓越的肖像画家。

Gu Kaizhi Draws a Picture of His Mother

Gu Kaizhi was a famous painter of the Eastern Jin Dynasty. He was good at drawing figures, especially women and fairies, and he could always depict the facial expressions with special skills to make it look very vivid. This was closely associated with his love and utter devotion to his mother.

Gu's mother died soon after he was born. He was left to his grandmother for care. As he looked strong and vivacious like a little tiger, the family all called him Tiger. His father used to be an imperial court official, but when he saw the darkness and corruption of politics, he retired to stay at home writing poems and articles. Gu Kaizhi would often rush into his father's study, asking, "Everyone has their mother. Where is mine? "

"Tiger, your mom has gone to her mother's far away from home." Afraid to upset his son, his father had to lie to him.

"Then when is she coming back? " He asked with eyes wide open.

"In about six months." His father told him.

From then on, Gu Kaizhi counted his fingers and was eagerly looking forward to his mother's return. Six months passed and he asked his father again. Seeing that he could no longer cover up the bad news, he told him all about his mother.

Learning that his mother already passed away, Gu Kaizhi couldn't help crying. His father comforted him, "Son, dead people cannot be restored to life. Your mother is gone. Don't think too much about this."

From then on, Gu became a person of few words, only imagining in his heart how his mother looked. He asked his father again and again about his mother's appearance and her figure. His father described her appearance. He then went to ask his grandmother. From this information, he gradually formed in his mind an image of his mother.

At eight, he said to his father, "I am going to draw a picture of my mother."

His father shook his head, saying, "You have never seen your mother before. How can you draw her picture? It won't look the same."

Gu didn't give up. He devoted his whole mind to drawing the picture of his mother, and when he finished the first one, he went to ask his father if the image looked close.

"No. It looks nothing like your mother." His father shook his head.

Then Gu drew a second picture and got the same answer. He drew again. When he drew the tenth picture, his father said,

"These look right, the shape of her body, hands and feet. But the face isn't."

Gu Kaizhi felt very happy, as if he had drank a glass of honey. He said to himself, "I will finally see my mother one day." He spent another six months drawing his mother and then showed it to his grandma. His grandma was afraid that he would tire himself out from drawing, so she said, "It looks like your mother now, Tiger. You can stop."

Gu didn't believe it and went to his father, who nodded, "Good, good. Only the expression in your mother's eyes doesn't look the same."

From then on, he concentrated on drawing the eyes. He drew and improved and drew again. After a period of time, he showed another picture to his father. To his great surprise, his father felt his wife was appearing before him, "This is really your mother." His father said. "Let's put it up on the wall."

Gu Kaizhi became a very famous portrait painter at the age of 20. When asked where he learned painting, Gu said, "My mother is always a living teacher in my heart."

【Comment】

Complete sincerity can affect even metal and stone. With his great love and devotion to his mother, Gu Kaizhi became an outstanding portraitist.

花木兰替父从军

花木兰是我国古代一名女英雄，她替父从军的故事流传千古。

木兰出身在北魏后期毫郡谯县（今河南商丘）的一户农家，父母都已年老，靠她和姐姐织布为生。木兰小时曾跟着父亲念过几年书，除了织布，她还爱骑马射箭，练得一身好武艺。

那时北方少数民族屡屡侵犯中原，战事频繁，人民生活极不安定。

一天，木兰一人在家织布，突然闯进几个差役，送来衙门发下的征兵军帖，要木兰父亲去应征当兵。差役走后，木兰心里一直不能平静：父亲已年过半百，怎能去打仗？弟弟又太小，根本不懂事。怎么办呢？木兰愁得连织布也没有心思……

不一会儿，父亲从外边回来，听不到木兰房中那熟悉的穿梭声，却传来女儿的阵阵叹息。他走进机房，问女儿："兰儿，你怎么啦？身体不好就别织布了。"

木兰见父亲问她，连忙打起精神回答："爹，我没怎么。昨天我看到衙门布告，刚才衙门里又送来军帖，爹已列入应征名单。"说着把一份军帖递给爹。见爹拿着军帖低头不语，木兰

木蘭從軍圖

拋下紅繡裳
換上青戎裝
替父去從軍
美名天下揚

笑求春月畫民間敬老故事

邢振齡並詩

接着说，"我想来想去，木兰没有兄长，弟弟又年小，女儿想代爹去从军，又舍不得离开爹娘……"

"兰儿，你真是一个孝顺女儿……但你是个女子，怎能从军呢？招兵的怎会收留一个女孩呢？"

"我想过了，可以女扮男装！"

父母知道女儿决定了的事很难改变，但他们怕女儿受不了行军打仗之苦，心里实在舍不得她走。

木兰含泪拜别父母，踏上了征途。

木兰是一个勇敢坚强的女子，她很快习惯了军队生活，一心在战场上杀敌立功。

行军作战的艰苦，木兰都能忍受，她害怕的是自己女扮男装的秘密被人识破，所以处处加倍小心。白天行军，她动作迅速，从不掉队；夜晚宿营，她和衣而卧，不脱军装；遇见敌军，她冲杀在前，毫不退缩。转眼10个年头过去了，没有人知道她是女儿身。

战争终于结束了，队伍凯旋，朝廷对将士们依功奖赏。木兰屡建战功，但她既不想做官，又不要财物，她只希望赏给她一匹快马，好早日回家和父母亲人团聚。上司满足了她的要求，并且派木兰的同伴护送她回家。

木兰千里迢迢回到家乡，一家人高兴极了。父母相互扶持着到城外迎接女儿回来，阿姐和小弟杀猪宰羊，准备酒席。

木兰回家头一件事便是到自己的闺房里脱下战袍，换上昔日的女儿装，梳理好姑娘发辫，还贴上金色的花黄饰品。当她走出房间向同伴道谢时，同伴大吃一惊："啊！同行12年，想不到你木兰竟是个女子哟！"

木兰替父从军的事迹传开以后，当地的人们编成歌谣赞颂她，夸她是爱国家、孝双亲的女英雄。至今，在河南虞城周庄村南郊还保存着一座木兰祠，每年四月初八，乡亲们常来此地纪念这位古代的孝烈女子。

【点评】

木兰替父从军的故事流传千古而不衰。从木兰身上我们看到，孝敬父母，赡养老人，男儿女儿是一样的。

Hua Mulan Joins the Army in Place of her Aged Father

Hua Mulan was a heroine in ancient China. The story about her joining the army in the disguise of a man in place of her father has been passed on from generation to generation.

Hua Mulan was born to a farmer's family in the town of Jiao of Hao County (now Shangqiu of Henan Province) during the late period of the Northern Wei Dynasty. Her parents were old and Mulan and her sister supported the family by weaving cloth. When she was young, she learned to read and write from her father. Apart from weaving cloth, she was good at riding, arrow-shooting, and especially martial arts. At that time, a minority group from north of China often invaded the country. There were many battles and people led an unstable life.

One day Mulan was weaving alone at home when some soldiers from the government office broke into the house. They left a military note that drafted her father to the army. After they left,

Mulan felt uneasy. "My father is over 50, too old to fight. My brother is still too young. What should I do?" Mulan was very worried, and she stopped weaving.

A while later, Mulan's father came back. He didn't hear the familiar weaving sound but his daughter's sighs instead. He walked in and asked, "Lan, what's wrong? You can rest if you don't feel well."

Seeing her father back, Mulan cheered herself up and answered, "Dad, I am fine. Yesterday I saw the bulletin from the government office, and just now they sent the military draft note. You are on the list." Saying this, Mulan passed her father the note. He said nothing. Mulan continued, "I already thought about it. I don't have older brothers and my younger brother is still young. I want to join the army for you, but I don't want to leave you..."

"Lan, you are a great daughter with filial piety. But, you are a girl. You cannot join the army. They won't take you."

"I have a plan. I can disguise myself as a boy."

Her parents knew that Mulan wouldn't change her mind once she made her decision. But they were also worried that Mulan couldn't withstand the sufferings in the army. They just couldn't bear to let her go.

Mulan said goodbye to her parents with tears in her eyes and set off.

Mulan was a strong and brave girl. She got used to the military life very soon and put all her mind into fighting for her country.

Mulan could bear all the hardships in the army as a soldier. What she feared most was that people would recognize her as a woman. She watched everything in order not to reveal anything particular as a woman. When her troop was on the march, she followed close; when camping at night, she slept with her uniform on; when meeting the enemy, she charged in front. In a flash ten years passed. No one ever found out Mulan was a woman.

Finally the war was over and the victorious army returned. The imperial court gave rewards to soldiers according to their merits. Mulan distinguished herself many times in battles, but she didn't want either the official rank or the money. She just asked for a speedy horse so that she could get back home to be with her family. Her superior agreed and sent her companions to escort her home.

The whole family was very happy to hear Mulan was coming back from afar. Her parents supported each other and walked to the city gate to welcome their daughter. Her sister and brother killed the pig and goat and prepared a feast.

The first thing Mulan did after she returned home was to change from her uniform to her clothes. Then she combed her hair, put on some makeup, and added a golden flower. When she walked out of her room to thank her companions, they were all startled, "Ah! We have been in the army with you for 12 years and never knew that you were a woman!"

The news of Mulan's exploit spread, and people compiled songs to eulogize her, praising her love of her country and filial piety to her parents. After her death, the local people built a memorial temple in her honor, which has been kept up to now south of the rural area of Zhouzhuang Village of Yu Cheng City in Henan Province. On the eighth day of the fourth month (lunar calendar) every year, local people will converge on the temple to pay homage to the heroine.

【Comment】

The story about Hua Mulan's joining the army in place of her father has been passed on from generation to generation. In her, we see that men and women are the same in respecting their parents.

孙思邈为双亲治病

唐初著名医学家孙思邈用毕生精力研究医药学，所著《千金方》记载了800多种药物和3000余个药方，史称"药王"。

谁会想到这位药王最初的学医动机竟是为了给父母治病。

孙思邈出生于陕西耀县一个贫苦家庭，父亲是一名木匠。他7岁时，父亲得了雀目病（即夜盲症），母亲患了粗脖子病。有一次，父亲锯木时，他在一旁看着发呆。父亲问他："孩儿，你长大了也要做木匠？"

"不，我不想做木匠。"

"那你想干什么？"

"我要做一名郎中，好给父母亲治病。"

父亲见他一番孝心，心里十分感动，就对他说："要当一名郎中就要去读书，不能像我这样一字不识，明天我就带你去念书。"

第二天，父亲陪着孙思邈到城外一座土窑里去当学徒。孙思邈见院子里里外外堆着许多草药，十分高兴，心想：要是在这些草药里能找到治父母亲病的药，就太好了！在此后的3年间，他经常向师父问这问那，常常使师父感到为难。后来，他知道师父只会用一些土方治病，根本不懂得药理，师父也知道徒弟的心思，就对他说："你聪明好学，我不能耽误你的前程。从这里北去40里的铜官县有一位名医，是我的舅舅，你到他那里去学医吧！"说完，送给他一本《黄帝内经》。

孙思邈到了铜官，找到了这位名医。在他那里一边学习，一边研究《黄帝内经》，医学知识长进不少。但这位名医也不知道如何治雀目病和粗脖子病，这使他十分失望。

第二年，孙思邈回到家乡开始给乡亲们治病。他行医不贪求财物，对病人同情爱护，渐渐地在家乡有了名声。有一次，他治好了一位病人的痼疾，病人到他家来答谢，得知孙思邈父母也身患痼疾，就对孙思邈说："我听说太白山麓有一位叫陈元的老郎中能治你母亲的那种病。"孙思邈一听大喜过望，第二天就去了太白山。孙思邈走了半个月终于打听到陈元郎中，陈元见他一片孝诚之心，就收他为徒弟。在陈元那里，孙思邈学到了治粗脖子病的祖传秘法，可是如何治雀目病仍毫无头绪。

一天，孙思邈问师父："为什么患雀目病的大多是贫苦人家，而有钱人家却很少得这种病？"

陈元听后说："你的话很有道理，不妨给病人多吃点肉食试试。"

孙思邈按照师父的话，要一位病人每天吃几两肉，但病人试了一个月毫不见效。于是他再翻阅大量医书，终于找到"肝开窍于目"的解释，就给那位病人改吃牛羊肝，不到半个月果然见效。孙思邈回家后立即用在太白山学到的方法给父母治病，不久他父母患的雀目病和粗脖子病都痊愈了。

【点评】

为父母治病的孝心，使孙思邈成为名垂史册的"药王"。爱的力量，多么伟大！

Sun Simiao Cures
His Parents' Diseases

Sun Simiao was a noted doctor in the early Tang Dynasty. He spent his whole life studying medicine and wrote Thousand Ducat Formulas, which recorded more than 800 kinds of medicines and more than 3,000 prescriptions, for which he was called the "King of Medicine."

But it is little known that he learned medicine at the beginning for the purpose of curing the diseases of his parents.

Sun was born to a poor family in Yao County of Shaanxi Province. His father was a carpenter. When he was seven years old, his father contracted night blindness while his mother suffered from goiter. One day, he stood aside staring blankly when his father was sawing the wood. His father asked, "Son, do you want to be a carpenter when you grow up? "

"No. I don't want to be a carpenter."

"What do you want to do then? "

"I want to be a doctor so that I can cure you and my moth-

唐代著名医学家，少年时为
拜名医为师，并为父母求医
问药，他翻山越岭，徒步四百多
里路，感动了老师而收他为徒
被史称药王，他就是
孙思邈。

er's diseases."

His father was very moved by his filial piety. He said, "If you want to be a doctor, you have to learn things first. You cannot be like your father, who doesn't even know how to read and write. Tomorrow I will take you to a doctor."

The next day, his father sent him to a cave dwelling in the rural area to learn medicine. Seeing piles of herbs in the yard, Sun felt very glad, thinking, "What if I could find right here the herb that could cure my parents' diseases! " During the next three years, he asked many questions, which often made his master embarrassed. Later he learned that his master only knew how to use some folk recipes and didn't know anything about pharmacology. His master knew what Sun wanted to learn, so he said to him, "You are very smart, and I cannot ruin your future. My uncle is a very famous doctor in Tongguan County, which is 20 kilometers away in the north. You can go to him." Then his master gave Sun a book called Huang Di Neijing (The Yellow Emperor's Canon of Internal Medicine).

Sun went to Tongguan and found the doctor. There Sun learned medicine from his new master and studied the medical book Huang Di Neijing. He made great progress. But the doctor didn't know how to treat the diseases of his parents either, which made Sun very disappointed.

The next year Sun returned home to give medical treatment to his country folks. During his medical practice, Sun cared about his patients with compassion and didn't covet wealth. Soon he made his name in his hometown. Once, he cured one of his patients of his chronic illness. The patient came to thank Sun. When he learned that Sun's parents had chronic illnesses too, he told Sun, "I heard that at the foot of the Taibai Mountain there is an old doctor called Chen Yuan, who can cure your mother's disease." Hearing this, Sun was very pleased and set off to the Taibai Mountain the next day. Sun spent half a month asking about Chen Yuan, who was moved by his piety and finally took him as an apprentice. There he mastered the secret recipe handed down for generations for curing goiters. But there was no solution to his father's night blindness.

One day Sun asked his master, "Why do only poor people suffer from such a disease, but rich people don't? "

Chen Yuan answered, "You are quite right. Why don't you try asking your patients to eat more meat? "

Sun followed his advice and made one of his patients eat more meat every day. But one month passed and there was no result. Then he read lots of medicinal works and found the interpretation that there was a close relation between the liver and the eyes. So he suggested that the patient eat livers of sheep and cattle. It took less than half a month before it worked. Returning from the Taibai Mountain, Sun treated his parents with what he had learned and soon his parents' diseases were both gone.

【Comment】

For the purpose of curing his parents' diseases, Sun Simiao became the "King of Medicine." This comes out of the power of love. How great it is!

唐代詩人白居易他為官一任敬老四方深得黎民愛戴每離任時鄉親們重重相送揮淚惜別

癸未春天畫敬老故事 邢振齡並題

白居易尊老敬老

　　唐代著名诗人白居易一生热爱祖国，关心百姓，特别关爱老年人。

　　白居易曾任江州（今江西九江市）司马，忠州（今四川忠县）、杭州、苏州等地刺史。他每到一个地方，总是让手下的官员先找来本地一些德高望重的老人，倾听意见，以便制定地方的施政方略。公务之余，白居易常简装便服，到百姓中听取他们的街谈巷议。听到一些老人遭受子女虐待的事，白居易特别生气，立即派人将这些不孝子女传讯上来，以情理责之，直到他们口服心服地承认错误并答应一定要孝敬老人时，才放他们离去。

　　遇到一些贫困的老人前来求援，白居易热心接待，尽力周济他们。他任忠州刺史时，有一年冬天，一位因兵乱而流落到四川的老人前来找他。白居易见这位老人衣不遮体，饥寒交迫，当即送给老人寒衣和回家乡的路费。老人捧着这些礼物，眼泪纵横，千恩万谢。望着老人远去的背影，白居易心酸地吟道："八十泰翁老不归，南宾太守乞寒衣。再三怜得非他意，天宝遗民见更稀。"

　　忠州城内有一位以卖麻饼为生的老妪，因制作技术差，生意清淡，入不敷出，生活十分拮据。有一次，白居易路过老妪的店前，在与老妪攀谈中得知情况，非常同情。回去后，白居易花费了好几天的时间，创造了一种发酵麻饼的制作工艺，并向老妪传授，使她家很快摆脱了贫困。后来，这种麻饼盛名远扬，当地人因白居易晚年号"香山居士"，遂给这种麻饼取名为"香山蜜饼"。

由于白居易的德政深得人心，因此在他离任时，地方百姓都扶老携幼地倾城出来为他送行，许多得到白居易恩惠的老人更是痛哭流涕，依依难舍。白居易在离开苏州时，一些老人竟随舟送出10里之外。

白居易一生写下了几千首诗歌，其中有相当一部分是写老人题材的。如《江南遇天宝乐叟》是写宫廷老乐工的，《杜陵叟》是写老农夫的，《上阳白发人》是写老宫女的。这些诗歌都脍炙人口，流传至今。在这些充满血泪的诗歌中，饱含了白居易对穷苦、善良的老人们深切的同情和关怀。

白居易还曾专门就养老问题给唐朝皇帝上过一道奏疏。在奏疏中白居易提出：养老之道，不仅仅只是发给老人们一些衣帛和食物，更重要的是要使老人们生活在一个安定的社会，有个安居乐寿的生活环境。"牧以仁贤，慎其刑罚"，使老人们得以长寿；"不夺其力，不扰其时"，使老人们过上富足的生活："使老者事长，少者敬老"。这些见解，有其独到之处。

（文　陈伟华）

【点评】

为官一任，造福一方。如果为官者都能像白居易那样，尊老敬老，关心老年人的疾苦，帮助老年人排忧解难，自然会受到百姓拥戴。

Bai Juyi's Respect for the Elderly

Bai Juyi was a well-known poet of the Tang Dynasty. For his whole life, he loved his country and cared about people, especially the elderly.

Bai Juyi served as a local officer in Jiangzhou (today Jiujiang City in Jiangxi Province) and a local governor in Zhongzhou (today Zhong County of Sichuan Province), Hangzhou and Suzhou. Everywhere he went, he would have his underling look for some local elderly people with high prestige in order to hear their views so that he could make local policies and regulations. In his spare time, he would dress in casual clothes and go among the common people to hear what they were talking about. He would feel very angry when he heard some elderly people being maltreated by their children, and would bring them to court immediately. He then pointed out their wrongs and would let them go when they sincerely admitted their wrongs and promised to take good care of their parents.

Whenever he met with some poor elderly people who came to him for help, he would warmly receive them and do all he could to assist them. One winter day, while he was a local governor in Zhongzhou, an old man who strayed into Sichuan because of the war came to him for help. Seeing him poorly dressed and starving, Bai Juyi immediately gave him some clothes and money to help him back to his hometown. Holding the clothes, the old man gave him a thousand thanks, with tears in his eyes. Watching him walking away, Bai Juyi thought sadly, "The 80-year-old man can't go back home. He came to me for a coat to keep himself warm. I feel sympathy for him for his old age. People of such age are getting fewer and fewer."

In Zhongzhou, there was an elderly woman who made a living on selling sesame cakes. But due to her poor technique, she didn't have lots of business, and she lived a very hard life. Once when Bai passed her store, he talked with the woman and heard her story. He was very sympathetic with the old woman. After he returned home, he spent several days studying the technique of making the cakes. Then he taught the old woman the technique, which helped her out of poverty. Later on this kind of cake became famous and the local people named the cake "Xiangshan honey cake" after Bai Juyi's refined name "Xiangshan Lay Buddhist".

As Bai Juyi won popular support for his governance by virtue, the entire city he served poured out to see him off when he left the office. Many elderly people who had received his favor cried. When Bai Juyi left his office in Suzhou, some elderly people even followed his boat for over three miles to see him off.

Bai wrote several thousand poems in his life and a considerable part was in eulogy of the elderly. In his "Meeting in Jiangnan with the Old official music" he wrote about an old musician who worked in the imperial court. His "Old Man from Duling" was about an old farmer. His "The Grey-haired Woman of Shangyang" was about an old maid in the imperial palace. These poems were very popular and have been passed down from generation to generation. Many of his poems were overflowing with his sincere sympathy and care to poor and kind-hearted elderly people.

Once Bai Juyi submitted his proposals to the emperor on the issue of providing for the aged, saying that it would not be enough just to give them food and clothes; what was more important was to allow them to live in a secure society and a peaceful living environment. He suggested "running a country with benevolence and kindheartedness, and being considerate with punishment," which could help the elderly live longer. He also suggested "leaving old people in peaceful environments, without taking away what they own, which could make them a good living," and "helping the elderly do what they are skilled at and telling the young to respect the old." These proposals show his unique views on the elderly.

(Chen Weihua)

【Comment】

If all officials are like Bai Juyi, respecting the elderly and showing concern for their sufferings and helping them out of difficulties, they will be naturally loved by the people.

黄庭坚亲涤溺器

贵显闻天下，平生孝事亲；

亲自涤溺器，不用婢妾人。

北宋著名诗人黄庭坚，年轻时就考取了进士，后历任多种官职。他从师于苏东坡，与秦观等人一道被称为"苏门四学士"。他的书法也特别好，尤其是行书和草书，以其独特的风格而闻名，被书法界誉为"苏黄米蔡"宋代四大家的第二家。

黄庭坚一生显贵，名扬天下，家中生活自是无忧。但他物质条件越好，越注意孝顺父母。他认为，生活条件优裕了，对父母的孝心就不仅是物质上的，还应体现在精神上。

他作为当世的名人，来往的也大多是有地位、有名气的人。但不管什么人到家作客，他都事先禀告母亲，以示对母亲的尊重。客人送来礼物，他都先拿给母亲看，只要父母喜欢，先给父母留下。

黄庭坚从小有个习惯，每天早晨起床后，先到母亲房中问安，然后亲自为母亲洗涤便盆。虽然他后来当了官，母亲身边有丫环服侍，但他的习惯依然如故。有人知道后，对他说：

"你现在已是朝廷命官，老太太有丫环服侍，你怎么还做这些粗活?"

黄庭坚说："一个人不管当了多大的官，在父母面前永远是孩子。如果没有父母，哪来我这个人？又哪里有官？子女服侍父母，要像奴仆一样。我这样做，表示我的一切都是父母赐的，并不能因为地位的改变而改变。"

一席话说得对方连连点头，叹息说："山谷先生（黄庭坚自号山谷道人）真不愧是真孝子，一个人有才而又孝，这是天下少有的啊！"

（文　范又琪）

【点评】

官越大，敬老品德越不能丢。黄庭坚官高位显，不忘孝道，亲涤便器，难能可贵。

Huang Tingjian Washes His Mother's Bed Pan

In imperial court, famous in high rank,

All days filial to the parent;

Wash the bed pan for mother himself,

Rest the maidservant.

Huang Tingjian was a noted poet of the Northern Song period (a dynasty between 960–1127). He became a successful candidate in the highest imperial examinations when he was very young and was promoted to an array of official posts. He learned poetry from Su Dongpo, a very famous poet and was well known as one of the four most famous disciples of Su Dongpo. He was also good at calligraphy, especially the regular script and cursive script. Because of his own special style, he gained his reputation as second among the four famous calligraphers "Su, Huang, Mi and Cai" of the Song Dynasty.

As a high-ranking official, Huang was well known and lived

a comfortable life. But, the better he lived, the more attention he paid to his parents. He thought he should not only show his filial piety by satisfying his parents' material needs, but also by supporting their spiritual needs.

As a notable, he often socialized with those who were well-known and in high posistion. Whenever visitors came, however eminent they were, to show his respect, he would let his mother know. When guests left gifts, he would show them to his mother first, and whatever his parents were interested in, he would keep it for them.

From early childhood, he formed a habit of going into his mother's room to say "good morning" after he got up and then wash the bed pan for her. Although his mother was served by a number of housemaids after Huang became a senior official, Huang still kept the habit. Once he was asked, "Now you are an important official in the imperial court and your mother has maids to serve her. Why do you still do this dirty job? "

Huang said, "No matter how high-ranking an official is, he is always a child to his parents. Without parents, there would not be me or any official. Children should serve their parents just like housemaids. I am doing this because everything I have is from my parents. I will not change, though my position may."

Hearing this, the person nodded to show his agreement, sighing, "Master Valley (Huang called himself Valley Taoist) is a real son with filial piety. It is hard to find another person with both talents and filial piety like you! "

(Fan Youqi)

【Comment】

Even a high-ranking official should not relinquish the good virtue of respecting the old.   It is praiseworthy that Huang Tingjian washed his mother's bed pan even in senior official position.

岳飞敬师孝母

公元1103年，河南相州汤阴县因黄河决口，发生了一场大水灾。

那一年，岳家生了个男孩，孩子的父亲岳和见婴儿出生时天上飞来一只大鸟，就把孩子取名为"飞"，字鹏举。

岳飞从小孝顺父母，7岁就帮父亲下地干农活。劳动回来，岳飞在岳和的指点下刻苦读书，除了《左传》，他最喜读《孙子兵法》，并爱好武艺。他身体健壮，18岁时就能拉300斤的大弓。

这时，金兵已在北方入侵辽国，窥视中原，岳飞发誓要练成本领，杀敌保国，一天，岳飞听得汤阴县里有一位叫周侗的老人，武艺高强，尤其擅长弓箭，岳飞就去周侗处，要拜他为师。

周侗见岳飞来求师，便问他："好孩子，你要学箭法干什么？"

"学了箭法就能奔驰疆场，保卫国家。"岳飞抬起头来精神抖擞地回答。

周侗见站在面前的这个年轻人志向远大，心中十分喜爱，当即便收了这个徒弟。

岳飞在周侗的传授下，很快学会了一手好箭法。不久，周侗去世。岳飞心中十分难过，每逢初一、十五，他都要置备一些酒肉，到老师坟前祭奠。他没有钱，就把身边的衣服当了买供品。这件事被他母亲发觉了，要丈夫去询问他。岳飞生性沉默寡言，没有回答父亲的话，只是跪在父亲的面前。父亲觉得奇怪，就留心观察岳飞的行动。

到了初一那天，岳和见儿子出门去了，便悄悄地跟在他后面。只见岳飞来到周侗坟前，先在坟旁射了三支箭，再把供品放在墓前跪下叩头，十分悲伤。

父亲见岳飞祭扫完毕，就上前问他："你拜过不少老师学艺，为什么独要祭周老师父呢?"

岳飞回答说："老师在生前一个月里把他一生摸索的箭法都传授给我，还教我立身处世精忠报国的道理，他的恩情是我一生最难忘怀的。"

岳和听了，觉得儿子已长大成人，正是报效国家的时候，便对岳飞说："金国侵辽以后，即将入侵中原，当今国势日衰，东京正在招募新兵，你可愿意去从军?"

岳飞回答说："孩儿早有此意，并约好张宪、牛皋几位兄弟准备不日去东京。"

岳和听了大喜，便要妻子给儿子准备行装。

岳飞离家前见母亲神情有些伤感，便对母亲说："孩儿这次去东京，以后不能侍奉母亲了，请母亲给我背上刺几个字吧!"说完，岳飞脱下上衣跪下。岳母含泪在岳飞背上刺了"精忠报国"4个大字。

从此，岳飞走上了报国之途，经过10多年的沙场鏖战，屡建奇功，成为一代抗金名将。

【点评】

岳母刺字，世代流传。"精忠报国"，激励后人。一代名将，为人师表。敬师孝母，精神永存。

Yue Fei's Respect for His Teacher and His Filial Piety to His Mother

In 1103 AD, a disastrous flood of the Yellow River inundated much of Tangyin County in Xiangzhou Region, Henan Province.

That year, a boy was born to the Yue family. Since a big bird flew by at the time of his birth, the father Yue He named the baby Fei (which means "Flying"), but the boy was also officially known as Pengju.

Yue Fei showed filial piety to his parents at an early age. At seven, he helped his father with field work. After work, he studied very hard with his father's help. He loved to read historical books. Besides the book Zuo Zhuan, The Art of War by Sun Zi was his favorite. He was also fond of martial arts.

When he learned that the Jin army had invaded Liao and was about to reach the Central Plains, Yue Fei resolved to learn military skills to defend his country. One day, he learned that an old man named Zhou Tong was highly skilled in martial arts, especially in archery, so he went to see him and pleaded to learn from him.

Zhou Tong asked Yue Fei, "Young man, why do you want to learn archery? " "So I can defend our country after I master the skill of archery," he answered in high spirits.

Zhou Tong was very delighted to see that this young man had such high aspirations, so he immediately accepted him as a student.

Very soon, Yue Fei mastered the skill of archery. Before long, his teacher died, and Yue Fei was very sad. Every first and fifteenth day of each lunar month, he would prepare some wine and meat to present at his master's tomb. If he did not have money, he would pawn his clothes to buy the offerings. This was discovered by his parents, who became concerned. His father asked him what happened. He knelt in front of his father with no words. The father was very curious and was determined to find out the cause of his strange behavior.

On the first day of a lunar month, Yue He saw his son walking out of the house. He followed him quietly. Yue Fei visited Zhou Tong's tomb again. First, he shot three arrows in front of his teacher's tomb. Afterwards, he presented the offerings, and then he knelt down in front of the tomb sadly.

The father observed everything the son did, and asked Yue Fei why he did this.

"My teacher taught me all his skills one month before his

death and taught me how to defend the country," Yue Fei said. "I will never forget."

His father was assured that Yue Fei had already grown up and that it was time to send him to serve the country. So, the father asked Yue Fei, "The Jin army has invaded Liao, and they will soon invade the Central Plains. Our country needs more people to defend it. Dongjing is recruiting soldiers now. Would you like to join the army?"

Yue Fei answered, "I have made up my mind already. I have also invited my friends Zhang Xian, Niu Gao, and others to join the army with me. We will leave home for Dongjing in a few days."

Yue He was very happy at his son's response. He told his wife to get everything ready for their son.

Yue Fei noticed that his mother was sad. He said, "Mother, I am leaving for Dongjing and I can't be here with you. Would you please tattoo a few words on my back?" He took off his coat and knelt on the floor. With tears in her eyes, the mother inscribed four Chinese characters on his back—"jing zhong bao guo"—meaning "Serve the country with supreme loyalty."

He fought the enemy on the battlefields for more than ten years, achieved numerous notable merits, and finally became a famous general.

【Comment】

This story has been passed down from generation to generation and has inspired the people of China.   This famous general
set a good example by respecting his teacher and parents.   His
influence will live forever.

岳飛自幼習武
練功 當金國
侵遼進入中
原時 他慨然
從軍離家
前他請母親在
背上刺上 精忠報國
四個字以報父母之恩
師長之情 多為國盡
忠

母子情

朱元璋向老秀才赔礼

　　明太祖朱元璋的太子自幼娇纵放任，7岁时朱元璋给他请的3位老师都先后告辞，不愿给太子授课。为此，朱元璋心中十分烦恼。一天，丞相刘伯温向他推荐一位老秀才，说："此人年已七十但学识渊博，且为人刚直无私，可任太子的老师。"朱元璋说："只要能严教太子，年纪大些更好。"第二日，朱元璋便请老秀才进东宫，对太子说："你一言一行都要好好听从这位老师的指导，不得无礼！"说罢，唤过太子向老秀才行礼。

　　一日，老秀才要太子背诵一段《论语》，自己则闭目养神。太子背了两句就取出书来偷看。突然，老秀才站起身来抓住太子的耳朵要他跪下。太子哪里肯听，反而挥起小拳头打老师。老秀才大声喝道："大胆！"说完把太子双手反扭过来，一定要他跪下，太子硬是不肯跪。

　　朱元璋刚好经过东宫，见了这一情景便走到老秀才面前求情："看在朕的面上，饶他一次吧！"

　　老秀才沉着脸说："养不教，父之过；教不严，师之惰。陛下应该知道这个道理。"

　　朱元璋见老秀才不仅不领情，反而当着太子的面来教训自己，不禁勃然大怒，喊道："来人！把这老家伙关起来！"

事情传到马皇后那里，她觉得皇上为太子护短，居然惩罚起老师来，太不讲道理，决定去劝皇上认错。

傍晚，马皇后在与皇帝用膳时，先向朱元璋劝了几杯酒，然后说道："皇上过去在淮西时曾说过，世上有两种人最无私心，皇上还记得吗？"

朱元璋一时记不起来，笑着说："朕记不得了，还请娘娘讲吧！"

马皇后说："一个是医生，一个是老师。皇上曾说，哪个医生不愿为病人治好病，哪个老师不愿把学生教成才，是吗？"

朱元璋听出娘娘话中有话，便说："如果老师太蛮横无理，就不是好老师了。"

马皇后说："这位老秀才脾气是有些怪，但他对太子教得严完全是为了他好呀！玉不琢，不成器，如果太子长大了无知无识，大明的天下不就完了吗？"

朱元璋听了心里懊悔起来，表示要向老秀才赔礼道歉。

第二天，朱元璋和马皇后先把太子叫来，当面教训一番，然后三人来见老秀才。老秀才见了他们，背着身子，故意不理睬。

朱元璋说："您老人家不必再生气了，朕特地向您赔礼来了！"

老秀才这时才向皇帝跪下施礼，说道："老臣不敢，谢圣恩！"

朱元璋先请老秀才坐下，再命太子向老师跪下叩首认错。老秀才扶起太子后，走到书桌前写了"明王明不明，贤后贤不贤"10个大字。

马皇后见了递给皇上。朱元璋一看顿时睁着两眼愣住了。

马皇后笑着说："请老师吟给皇上听吧！"

老秀才吟道："明王明不？明。贤后贤不？贤。"

朱元璋一听哈哈大笑。

【点评】

"养不教，父之过。教不严，师之惰"。"玉不琢，不成器"。这些警世名言传至今日，仍有其现实意义。封建帝王朱元璋知错就改的态度值得称道。

Zhu Yuanzhang Apologizes to the Old Teacher

Zhu Yuanzhang, the first emperor of the Ming Dynasty, asked three teachers to instruct his spoiled 7-year-old son. None of them enjoyed teaching him, and they quit, one after another. Zhu Yuanzhang was very much distressed. One day, Prime Minister Liu Bowen recommended an old scholar and said, "Though he is over seventy, he is very knowledgeable, and he is strict and selfless. He should be a good candidate." Zhu Yuanzhang noted, "If he is strict in teaching, I don't mind his age." The next day, Zhu Yuanzhang invited the old scholar to the court. He introduced his son to the teacher and told the boy to obey the teacher and not to do anything rude. He urged his son to bow to his teacher.

One day, the old teacher asked the prince to recite a passage from the book The Analects of Confucius and closed his eyes, listening. The prince could not recite it and stole a glance at the book. Suddenly the old teacher seized the ear of the prince and ordered him to kneel. The prince refused and waved his fist at the teacher. "Bold child! " the old teacher said loudly. He snatched the boy's arms and twisted them behind his back, and again ordered him to kneel. The boy refused again.

Zhu Yuanzhang happened to pass by. He saw the scene and asked the teacher, "Please forgive him this time, for me."

The old teacher said to the emperor, "It is the fault of the father if his son is not well taught; it is the laziness of the teacher if the teaching is not strict. Your Majesty should know this truth."

The emperor was angered that the old man scolded him before his son, so he had the teacher put into custody.

When the Empress Ma learned this, she felt that the emperor had gone too far in punishing the teacher. She decided to persuade the emperor to apologize to the teacher.

At the dinner table, while Zhu Yuanzhang was content, she asked the emperor, "Do you still remember you once said that there were two kinds of people who were selfless? "

Zhu Yuanzhang could not recall. He responded with a smile to the empress, "I cannot remember. Please tell me."

The empress said, "One is a doctor; the other is a teacher. Your Majesty once said, 'The doctors strive to cure their patients, while the teachers strive to train their students to be useful people.' "

Zhu Yuanzhang argued, "If the teacher is very rude, then he is not a good teacher."

The empress added, "This old teacher does have a strange

temper, but his strictness is for the good of our son. Jade can not be turned into anything good without being cut and polished. If the prince grows into an ignorant person, there will be no successor to the Ming Dynasty."

Zhu Yuanzhang regretted his actions and decided to apologize to the teacher.

The following day, the emperor called his son and scolded him for his rudeness to the teacher. Afterwards, the royal couple and the prince went to see the teacher. When he saw them, the old teacher turned his back on them and paid them no mind.

Zhu Yuanzhang said, "Please do not be angry any more. We came here especially to apologize to you."

The old teacher was very touched. He knelt and said, " Thank you, Your Majesty."

Zhu Yuanzhang invited the old teacher to sit down, and asked his son to kneel in front of the teacher and apologize. After the old teacher helped his student up, he went to his desk and wrote the Chinese characters, "Is the Ming Emperor wise? Yes. Is the Empress understanding and gracious? Yes."

Hearing this, Zhu Yuanzhang laughed.

【Comment】

It is the fault of the father if a son is not filial; it is the laziness of the teacher if the teaching is not strict. Jade cannot be turned into anything good without being cut and polished. These famous Chinese aphorisms have been passed down until today and are still of practical significance. It is praiseworthy for the august emperor to correct the errors he had committed.

戚继光牢记父训

　　明代抗击倭寇入侵的民族英雄戚继光出身于世代将门之家。父亲戚景通是一位久经沙场、屡立军功的老将。56岁时才生下一子，取名继光。老将军晚年得子，对继光十分钟爱，但教子极严。

　　戚继光12岁时，有一天练武回到家中，见工匠们正在修理厅堂。一个工匠对他说："你家世代做官，戚将军功名不小，照例该造一间12扇雕花窗的大花厅，现在你父亲只修一间4扇窗的厅，未免太节省了。"

　　戚继光听后对父亲说："工匠说父亲官职不小为什么不修造一间雕花窗的大厅呢？"

　　父亲摇了摇头说："你小小年纪就贪慕虚荣，将来我这份产业到你手里怕保不住呢！你想想，工匠的话对不对？"

　　戚继光从小聪明，一下就明白了父亲话里的意思，回答说："孩儿听从父亲教诲，实在不该听工匠的话。"

　　第二年，家中要给戚继光定亲。女方家中送来一双非常昂贵的绣鞋，戚继光见了这双鞋，翻来覆去看不够。母亲说："看你这般喜爱，就拿去穿吧！"他穿上绣鞋走到父亲书房，高兴地问："父亲，你看这双鞋漂亮吗？"父亲一见皱起眉头，严肃地说："我上次为修大厅的事就对你说过，不要贪图享乐，你现在又犯了！一双绣鞋虽小，但如果你爱慕虚荣享受之心不改，将来当了将军不爱财不贪污才怪呢！"

戚继光听了红着脸，把绣鞋脱掉说："孩儿知错，这双鞋我决不再穿。"

父亲又问他："宋代岳飞曾说过什么话？"

"文官不贪财，武官不怕死，国家就兴旺。"

"对，你要终生牢记这句话！认真读书，苦练武艺，才能为国立功，干一番大事业！"

几年后，戚继光成为一名文武双全的青年军官。这时父亲正埋头著一部兵书，有人劝戚景通晚年要多置买些田产好留给后代，他听了对继光说："你知道父亲为什么给你取名继光吗？"

"要孩儿继承戚家军名，光耀门第。"

"继儿，我一生没有留给你多少产业，你不会感到遗憾吧！"

戚继光指着厅堂上父亲写的一副对联，"授产何若授业，片长薄技免饥寒；遗金不如遗经，处世做人真学问。"他读了一遍后说："父亲从小教我读书习武，还教我怎样做一个品德高尚的人，这是给孩儿最宝贵的产业，孩儿从未想到贪图安逸和富贵，我想早些看到父亲将来像岳飞建'岳家军'一样，创立一支'戚家军'。"

戚景通听了心中十分宽慰，笑着对儿子说："我这部兵书已经完成了，现在我要传给你。这是我一生的心血，将来你用它报效国家吧！"

戚继光跪在地上，双手接过这部《戚氏兵法》说："孩儿一定研读这部兵法，不管将来遇到什么艰难险阻，我也不会丢弃父亲的一生心血。"

戚景通在72岁时患重病去世，戚继光接到噩耗从驻防地赶回家中奔丧。他在父亲坟上哭着说："继光一定继承您的遗志，为国尽忠，赴汤蹈火，在所不辞！"

　　嘉靖三十四年，朝廷任戚继光为佥浙江都司，负责抗倭。他组织"戚家军"，在6年中九战九捷，威震中外。他曾对人说："我之能抗倭取胜，全靠我父亲在世的谆谆教诲啊！"

【点评】

　　教子重教德，敬老学做人。戚父教子不慕虚荣，其子遵父训不贪享乐。古人尚能做到，今人更当如此。

Qi Jiguang's Family Precepts

Qi Jiguang, a national hero of the Ming Dynasty, was born to a general's family. His father, Qi Jingtong, was a well-known general, who also achieved numerous notable merits in defending the country against enemy invasion. His son, Jiguang, was born when he was 56. He loved his son very much, but was very strict in family teaching.

When Qi Jiguang was 12, his family asked some repairmen to mend their reception hall. One day, the boy came home after his training. One of the men said to him, "Your family members have been officials for generations. General Qi has also accomplished so many meritorious achievements. You should build a bigger hall with twelve beautiful windows. This four-window hall is too small."

Qi Jiguang found his father and asked, "The repairman said that you are a high-ranking official; why can't we build a bigger hall? "

His father shook his head and said, "You indulge yourself with luxuries at such young age. I am afraid that you won't be a good successor after I die. Think it over. Is what the repairman said correct? "

Qi Jiguang was very bright and he immediately understood what his father meant. "I understand, Father. I should not listen to the repairman."

The following year, his family arranged a marriage for him and the bride-to-be sent him a pair of very beautiful and expensive shoes. Qi Jiguang loved them very much and put them on as his mother suggested. Wearing his new shoes, he strode into his father's study to show them off. Unexpectedly, his father frowned at him and said, "I told you last time not to indulge yourself with luxuries. Now you do it again. If you do not correct yourself, I doubt you will ever become a good general."

Flushed with shame for his vanity, Qi Jiguang took off the shoes and promised not to wear them again.

"Do you know what Yue Fei in the Song Dynasty once said? " the father asked him.

The son replied, "The country would grow prosperous if the civilian officials were not greedy for money and military officers did not fear death."

"Please remember these words forever. Study hard and practice constantly; then you can serve the country and make great achievements." the father added.

A few years later, Qi Jiguang became a young officer and was well versed in both polite letters and martial arts. At this time, his father immersed himself in writing a book on war. Some people advised the elder Qi to buy some property for his future generations. Hearing this, the father asked his son, "Do you know why I gave you name Jiguang? "

"You hope that I will cherish our family's military heritage and glory, " the son answered.

"Would you feel ashamed and pitiful if I don't leave you much property? " asked the father.

He then pointed to the wall at the couplet which his father had once written: "It is better to leave knowledge than property; it is better to leave teachings than money, " and responded, "You taught me how to read and trained me in the use of military weapons since I was young. You also taught me to be a decent man. This is more important than material wealth. Your son is not greedy for ease and wealth. I cannot wait to see our own Qi's military troop some day, just like Yue's of the Song Dynasty."

Qi Jingtong was very satisfied at his son's answer. With a smile, he told his son, "I have completed the book on the art of war. I will give it to you. I have put all my heart into writing it. I hope this book will be useful to you when you serve the country."

Kneeling down, Qi Jiguang took the book from his father with both hands and pledged, "I will study very hard and keep your book with me in all circumstances."

Qi Jiguang's father died of illness at the age of seventy-two. Qi Jiguang rushed home from the front. "I will carry on your will, and serve the country with loyalty, " he promised with tears in eyes.

In the 34th year of Jia Jing, Qi Jiguang was appointed commander of an army in Zhejiang, and his mission was to defend the country against invaders. He organized and led the Qi's army to victory in nine battles over a six-year period.

"I owe my victories to the teachings of my father," Qi said.

【Comment】

Family education stresses moral education. To respect the aged is to learn how to behave. Qi Jiguang's father taught him not to indulge in vanity, and Qi himself respected his father and never fell into the trap of greed and pleasure. The ancients could achieve this; why not people of the present-day world?

郑板桥责行孝道

郑板桥任山东潍县县令时，爱微服私访体察民情。一天，他领着一名书童走到城南一个村庄，见一民宅门上贴着一副新对联：

> 家有万金不算富；
> 命中五子还是孤。

郑板桥感到很奇怪，既不过年又不过节，这家贴对联干什么，而且对联写得又十分含蓄古怪。他便叩门进宅，见家中有一老者。老者强颜欢笑将郑板桥让进屋内。郑板桥见老人家徒四壁，一贫如洗，便问道："老先生贵姓？今日有何喜事？"老者唉声叹气说："敝姓王，今天是老夫的生日，便写了一副对联自娱，让先生见笑了。"郑板桥似有所悟，向老者说了几句贺寿的话，便告辞了。

郑板桥一回县衙，便命差役将南村王老汉的10个女婿叫到衙门来。书童纳闷，便问道："老爷，您怎知那老汉有10个女婿？"郑板桥给他解释说："看他写的对联便知。小姐乃'千金'，他'家有万金'不是有10个女儿吗！俗话说一个女婿半个儿，他'命中五子'，正是十个女婿。"书童一听，恍然大悟。

老汉的10个女婿到齐后，郑板桥给他们上了一课，不仅讲了孝敬老人的道理，还规定10个女婿轮流侍奉岳父，让他安度晚年。最后又严肃地说："你们中如有哪个不善待岳父，本县定要治罪！"第二天，10个女儿带女婿都上门看望老人，并带来了不少衣服、食品。王老汉对女婿们一下子变得如此孝顺，有点莫名其妙，一问女儿，方知昨日来的是郑大人。

【点评】

孝敬老人，不仅是家事，也是官员实行德政的重要内容。为官一方，不仅要以身作则，带头敬老，更要像郑板桥那样，责行孝道。

Zheng Banqiao Promotes the standards of Filial Piety

While he was a county magistrate in Shandong Province, Zheng Banqiao routinely went in disguise among the common people to observe the civil situation. One day, he took an attendant to a village and saw a new couplet on the doors of a house. The verse read:

The family still remains poor though it has "ten thousand jin (gold)";

Loneliness still prevails, though there are "five sons" around.

Zheng Banqiao was curious about this. It was neither the Spring Festival nor any other holiday, and the couplet was very implicative and strange, so he wondered why the family placed this couplet on the door at this time of the year. He knocked on the door and was invited into the house. He found nothing in it but an old man. "May I know your name? " asked the magistrate, "Are you celebrating an event today? "

The old man sighed and answered, "My name is Wang. Today is my birthday. I wrote this couplet to entertain myself." Zheng Banqiao seemed to understand the old man's situation. He congratulated the old man, and took his leave.

As soon as he returned to the county office, he ordered his servant to summon the ten sons-in-law of the old man. His attendant was puzzled and asked, "Your Excellency, how did you know that the old man had ten sons-in-law? " Zheng Banqiao answered, "I inferred it from the couplet. A girl is called 'one thousand jin,' and the couplet said the family had ten thousand jin, so the old man must have ten daughters. Again, there is an old saying, 'A son-in-law is a half-son,' and the couplet said that the family had five sons." The attendant suddenly saw the light by his explanation.

When the ten sons-in-law arrived at the county office, one after the other, Zheng Banqiao gave them a lecture on how to respect and show filial piety to older people. He made a ruling that the ten sons-in-law must take turns caring for their father-in-law and helping him enjoy his remaining years. He said seriously, "If any of you is disrespectful to your father-in-law, that son-in-law will be punished."

The following day, the ten daughters and ten sons-in-law all went to visit the old man, bringing food and clothing.

The old man was very surprised to see this. After asking his daughters, he realized that the man who had visited him the day

中华敬老故事精选

before was Zheng Banqiao.

【Comment】

Respecting the elderly is not only a family duty, but also an important part of governing with virtue. An official should not only set an example for others in respecting our elders, but also promote the standards of filial piety just as Zheng Banqiao did.

陈老汉贴对联

相传古代安徽某地有位陈老汉，年逾60岁，儿子却不尽赡养义务。陈老汉无奈，便向他的侄儿诉苦。

侄儿对他说："我自有办法。"说罢，回家写了一副对联和一幅中堂，要陈老汉贴在屋内正墙上。

那副对联的上联是："二三四五"；下联是："六七八九"。显而易见，这副对联缺"一"（衣）少"十"（食）。这幅中堂更耐人寻味，使人警悟，写的是：

"隔窗望见儿喂儿，想起当年我喂儿。

我喂儿来儿饿我，当心你儿饿我儿。"

儿子、媳妇见了，羞愧万分。从此痛改前非，父子言好。

【点评】

自己对父母的态度，是对子女最好的示范。期望子女孝敬自己，就要从自己孝敬父母做起。否则，发生"我喂儿来儿饿我"就是必然的。从这个意义上说，虐待父母，就是虐待自己。

Couplet

Legend has it that an old man named Chen lived in Anhui Province. He was over 60, but his son refused to perform his obligations to support him. The old man complained about this to his nephew.

His nephew said, "I have a good idea." So saying, he went home and wrote a couplet, each line on a separate scroll, and a central scroll, and asked the old man to hang them on the front wall in his house.

The couplet read: "two, three, four, five" and "six, seven, eight, nine." Apparently, "one" and "ten" were missing. In Chinese, the number "one" (yi) is pronounced like the sound of the Chinese character meaning "clothes," and "ten" (shi) is pronounced like the sound of the character meaning "food." The couplet indicated that he lacked food and clothing.

The central scroll read:

Through the window, I see my son feeding his son,

This reminds me of the time when I fed my son;

I fed my son but now my son is starving me,

Beware that your son would starve my son.

When the old man's son and daughter-in-law saw this, they felt very ashamed. From then on, they were determined to correct past mistakes and treat their father well.

【Comment】

One's attitude toward parents is a good demonstration for children. If you expect your children to show filial care to you, you must show the same to your parents. Otherwise, the case of "I fed my son but now my son is starving me" would be inevitable. In this sense, to mistreat your parents is to maltreat yourself.

隔窗望見兒喂兒
想起當年我喂兒
我喂兒來兒餓我
當心你兒餓我兒
畫民間責兒不孝流传的順口溜故事

图书在版编目（CIP）数据

中华敬老故事精选/李宝库主编 .—北京：中国社会出版社，
2004.12
ISBN 7 – 5087 – 0357 – X

Ⅰ.中... Ⅱ.李... Ⅲ.英语—对照读物，故事—英、汉
Ⅳ.H319.4：Ⅰ

中国版本图书馆 CIP 数据核字（2004）第 126779 号

书　　名：中华敬老故事精选
主　　编：李宝库
副 主 编：陆　颖
特约编辑：邢开敏　柴　火
策划编辑：李　凝
责任编辑：张博超

出版发行：中国社会出版社　　　邮　编：100032
通联方法：北京市西城区二龙路甲 33 号新龙大厦
　　　　　电　话：66051698　电　传：66051713
　　　　　欢迎读者拨打免费热线：8008108114
　　　　　或登录 www.bj114.com.cn 查询相关信息
经　　销：各地新华书店

印刷装订：中国电影出版社印刷厂
开　　本：787×1092 毫米　1/16
印　　张：16.5
字　　数：200 千字
版　　次：2004 年 12 月第 1 版
印　　次：2004 年 12 月第 1 次印刷
书　　号：ISBN 7 – 5087 – 0357 – X/H·83
定　　价：98.00 元
